STOP THE BLEEDING

STOP THE BLEEDING

BRIAN SANDS

ABOUT BRIAN SANDS

Brian Sands is a business problem solver, as an interim executive leading organisational change, and as a strategy advisor to boards and executive teams managing risk. His insights have been gained through frontline hands-on and hands-in experience in large-scale, high-risk, low-margin construction and property businesses. He has a unique background through every role from labourer to managing director, from carpentry apprenticeship to masters degree, from subcontractor to significant business owner.

This opportunistic mindset gained considerable traction in the early 2000s when as managing director and major shareholder he grew a construction business from $34M to more than $100M over four years without external capital or shareholder equity, and then at the height of the GFC and deep inside a multi-million-dollar turnaround, created a $250M joint venture with a subsidiary of one of the world's largest contractors. During this period his business constructed more than $1B in projects, succeeding through growth, transformation, joint-venture and turnaround strategies.

Brian's advisory portfolio experience is approaching $2B in managed value, including global expansion, exit restructuring, property development, dispute management and start-up business. He is a non-executive director, managing director, general manager and independent advisor with over 20 years of board-level experience across commercial and not-for-profit sectors.

GRATITUDE

Life in general, and indeed anything that gets thrown at you along the way, is hardly rewarding or meaningful without trusted relationships and authentic connections.

I am sincerely grateful for the unconditional support of my family, the positive influence of my mentors and friends, and the authentic experiences gained alongside my colleagues and clients.

Thank you, Mum and Dad, for the hard-work ethic and problem-solver DNA that our family is lucky to *own*. And thanks for the freedom of always allowing me to make my own decisions during my formative years – good, bad and otherwise! The ability to 'back myself' in decision-making that this freedom has provided is the foundation of my independence and drive.

Mim, thank you seems inadequate. I am so grateful that you ensured our life outside of business is always unconditionally loving, fun, and all about family. I know I am very lucky to do life with you. My running mate. My sounding board. My people coach. My renovation co-worker. My tour guide. My wife. Thank you. xxx

Jess, Liv and Lucy, I am extremely proud of you three. My 'mad chicks'. Thank you for being independent, intelligent, resilient and respectful, in spite of my Dad jokes! As a parent, seeing you succeed and be genuinely good people makes the hard slog worthwhile.

I am so excited about what lies ahead for you, although I get the feeling that you may have it covered already. xxx

In memory of and thanks to my grandfather, Jack Stone, or Pa Jack as he was affectionately known, my first official business partner 30 years ago who passed away at age 96, the year I was writing this. He had a tough life but never had a chip on his shoulder. He worked very hard for a very long time. His advice to us kids to 'keep on punching' I am sure was his mantra throughout his own life. To keep going, to never give up, to get it done. Someone who never said a bad word about anyone, always reminding us to 'let the other person make the mistake'. A wonderful man. A great role model.

Marc Stigter, I cannot thank you enough for turning the light on 14 years ago, teaching me to see, think, plan and act differently every day – from being my Melbourne Business School program director, to our APM Group strategy advisor, to being my mentor for years, and all throughout, my friend. Somehow you made being deep in the frontline turnaround trenches and under heavy fire exciting. You have always pushed my thinking, and you have contributed greatly to my learning, and to this book. Thank you Mate.

Post-GFC when our back was to the wall and we were bleeding cash, closing the door was a real possibility. I will be forever grateful to you David Marriner for the seven-figure advance on little more than a handshake. You were a client and you could have walked away. Without this we were history, and everything since would have been fundamentally different. I appreciate the authentic friendship that we have to this day. Thank you David.

To my good buddy Paul McMurtrie, thank you for your energy and your excitement, and for teaching me that disaster is only a 'sub-optimal' situation. You have left us way too early my friend, and subtle mentor. I can't thank you enough for rewiring my opportunity radar.

I really appreciate, and cannot recommend highly enough, the incredible guidance and high-quality input from Michael Hanrahan and Anna Clemann and their Publish Central behind-the-scenes team. I really thought that this was going to be the difficult piece, however the way in which the edit, design and layout aligned with the context and content exceeded my expectations. Thank you.

Perhaps not unlike an artist hanging a painting in a gallery exposing themselves to critique and opinion, writing a book as an inexperienced author is high risk. In addition to not only committing valuable time to reading and sense-checking my perspectives, thank you Kath Walters for your initial manuscript review, as you say – helping me build the plane as I fly it; John Good for your international people management experience; Peter Jackson for your considered thought around the chronology of a turnaround mindset; Tony Peake for your detailed review of the key people leadership considerations; St John Frawley for your high-value red pen and structured thought; and Dr Janine Cooper for your technical neuroscience perspective and thorough feedback. With all of your help I feel that my risk has been mitigated somewhat.

To my clients, thank you for the privilege of working inside your organisations, for trusting me with your business and your people, and for enabling me to continue to learn with you.

Finally, thank you, my reader, for being interested in how to *Stop The Bleeding*.

Project management and text design by Michael Hanrahan Publishing
Cover design by Peter Reardon

Disclaimer

CONTENTS

CONTENTS

FOREWORD

When there's a leak in your boat, the first priority clearly is to stop it. When your organisation is 'bleeding' value as a result of today's troubled and uncertain conditions, the first priority equally is to stop-the-bleeding. But *how* exactly do you do this? Or, as Brian Sands puts it: 'Where are the textbooks that specifically lay out how to achieve this?' Well, here it is!

Stop the Bleeding offers you a pragmatic guide showing not only how to reset your business today but also how to do more and better enduringly into the future. In my view, this book goes beyond 'just' stopping-the-bleeding and takes you on a practical journey of reimagining and renewing your business.

At the core of *how* to do this, Brian Sands invites you – as a leader – to see, think, plan and act ... DIFFERENTLY. 'It is only through a journey of different thinking that you will unlock your ability for different doing,' he says. From my own experiences, this takes courage.

For us as leaders to see and think differently, we need the courage to question our own ingrained thinking and practices first. Daring to question your own leadership habits is not that easy. As we all know, old habits do die hard. Especially, when these habits have been successful in the past and consequently have become part of our leadership identity. Success in the past always becomes enshrined in the present by the over-valuation of the thinking and practices which accompanied that success. We as leaders unconsciously start holding on to these past successes that have become business-as-usual. We unconsciously become consumed with 'protecting' the status quo.

And here lies our biggest risk, as the author of this book so righty highlights. Since we are what we repeatedly do, we can easily become stereotyped creatures, imitators and copiers of our past selves, as philosophised by William James in the 19th century. The one thing that we can all presume is that stereotyped thinking and practices won't be moving-the-needle in this century. A century in which we already have encountered two unprecedented global economic crises within the first two decades alone. This is why Brian Sands calls for a mind shift of today's business leaders and invites you to see and think differently. He offers 'simple' tips as how to embrace a don't-look-back mindset and free yourself up to think differently about your leadership practices and your organisation's desired state.

In the end, *Stop the Bleeding* is a leadership book and in a way the author takes you back to the essence of this concept. In this no-nonsense book, Brian Sands gets rid of all the drama and all the leadership rhetoric. He distils all the hoopla down to nuts and bolts and reminds you what 'leadership' is ultimately all about.

And frankly, we all do need reminding. Because what many of us seem to have forgotten – both in theory and in practice – is that leadership ultimately is about *direction*. The Anglo-Saxon etymological root of the words 'lead, leader and leadership' is *laed*, which means path or road. So, the second we call ourselves 'leaders', we can't just be consumed with 'managing' day-to-day operational issues, we equally need to be consumed with realising our preferred road or path or direction through people. Realising a preferred direction or vision means automatically realising some sort of strategic change.

Stop the Bleeding is a compelling 'play book' as how to strategically change your business in a period of uncertainty. It is a blueprint for any level of leadership looking to do more and better both personally and organisationally in testing times. The book blends theory with practice in the context of Brian Sands' own professional and personal experiences. This gives *Stop the Bleeding* practical relevance and deep authenticity. As Brian Sands sincerely reveals: 'I go deep in places, and I am willing to do so because not only did I learn plenty from these experiences, I hope you might stretch your thinking also.'

Stop the Bleeding, therefore, is a genuine invitation to also be courageous, to dare to go deep and to stretch your thinking as a leader. All that remains for me to say within this foreword – and in a typical Brian Sands' energetic way – is: 'Game on!'

Marc Stigter PhD
Award Winning Author

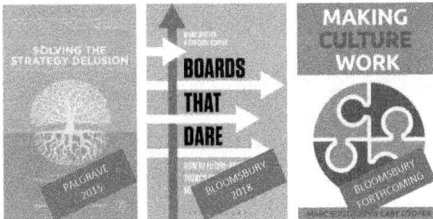

INTRODUCTION
DEAD MEN CAN'T PAY
SCHOOL FEES

Having reversed down the bluestone laneway at the back of our inner-city house, slowly idling through the carpark so as to not wake the neighbours, I considered it odd that there were a couple of guys on motorbikes just parked there. It was 6.30am. But I didn't think too much of it.

It was early 2010, and our construction business had moved on from the depths of the Global Financial Crisis a year or so earlier, or so we thought. When it did impact us a few years later it took us three years to fully overcome.

What the GFC brought to the construction industry was a new normal that halved contractor margins to very low single figures and redefined business sustainability to maintaining short-term cashflow rather than retaining earnings for growth. It created a transient workforce as people looked to shore up their livelihoods. At the next level down, the reduced projects, increased competition and a reliance on monthly cashflows was cleaning out subcontractors at a fast rate. The fight for market share, the competition for cashflow and the concerns around the fundamentals of livelihood had created an increasingly aggressive environment.

The post-stimulus music had stopped.

The day before seeing these guys on their bikes, I had taken a call from a well-known insolvency partner. It was an unusually formal call as we were on a first-name basis, however I soon understood why. He told me that an electrical subcontractor he represented had gone into liquidation because my company owed them $9 million. This was wrong: we now thought that the contractor was a crook. It was alleged by many that he had a drug problem, he was stealing from his own company, ripping off his parents, installing non-compliant products and delaying our projects. I explained all this and more in one breath and hung up.

In the following 24 hours another one of our subcontractors hit the wall, a heating and air-conditioning firm. As a result, we now had an unjustified combined total of $10M alleged against us.

I soon had clients on the phone asking if we were next, with each wanting to meet me urgently to assess our solvency and be convinced of our strategy to complete their projects. Fair enough; I was trying to find those answers myself. I was navigating deep and unchartered waters, and the sharks were circling.

The next morning, I followed the same 6.30am routine. And as with the day before, there were a couple of guys on motorbikes sitting in the carpark.

This time I thought more of it.

At the office the phone didn't stop. Clients, project managers, subcontractors, staff and others. One particular call was quite confronting, to say the least. It was a private number, and all the caller said was, 'You must have plenty of money to send your girls to that private school.'

Needless to say, this gave me quite a scare. For a few days I lost a bit of focus. From that point, my business survival mindset had just ratcheted up a few notches to now be consumed with protecting my family. I couldn't tell – or rather didn't want to worry – my wife. I just had to deal with this ... somehow. The problem was that I hadn't worked out how. Or who. Or what. So I said nothing.

I stayed up all night that night. Our bedroom was upstairs over the laneway, so if I left the window open I would know when these carpark visitors arrived, still optimistically thinking that their presence was just a coincidence. I must have fallen asleep at some stage, as my biker friends had returned the next morning without me realising.

I can't remember how long this went on for, but I think it was when they appeared about sleep-deprived day five that I jumped out of my idling car and started ranting at them, along the lines of, 'Are you looking for me? ... What do you want? ... ' And in a desperate act that appears comical in hindsight, I attempted to hand one of them a business card and shouted at them to 'come and see me in my office'. Funny now I know, but I was trying to get them away from my family, despite them obviously knowing where I lived. They rode away – maybe due to all the noise I had created.

This all might sound like bravado, but it wasn't. I was very worried.

The phone calls were relentless, every day. We were in deep now. The pipeline had dried up, competition had intensified, our reputation was suffering, our contractors were desperately aggressive, and we were bleeding cash.

Later that same day I received a random phone call: 'Dead men can't pay school fees.'

MY JOURNEY

This intense, aggressive and threatening period was the start of a frightening, and then exciting, journey in doing leadership differently. By differently, I mean compared to what we might perceive to be a traditional and perhaps passive evolution of skills among a hierarchy of management.

Traditionally, managing a business is learnt on the job, usually in an active rather than aggressive and distressed market – we experience, we learn, we succeed, we fail, and we progress, in no particular order. We can also learn business management sitting in a classroom 'listening' to the academic approach that informs traditional business planning, financial analysis, sales and marketing, and human resources, for example.

Or we can do both.

I have benefited from a considerable amount of education, yet nearly everything I know has been learnt on the job; it has been a continuous cycle of experience and learning that each time enhances the exposure to equally advancing risk and opportunity. One provided knowledge, the other know-how.

To complement these learnings, the bridge between education and experience was built alongside some great mentors to whom I remain extremely grateful.

As a managing director and major shareholder, I have successfully co-created exponential growth through turnaround, transformation and joint-venture strategies leading a business that constructed more than $1B in projects.

As an advisor, my current portfolio is closing in on $2B intervention value, including global expansion strategies, exit restructuring, dispute management, property development and start-up business strategies.

I started out as a builder's labourer and then completed a carpentry apprenticeship. By 25 I was managing more than 400 construction workers up and down the east coast of Australia, before setting up a business in New Zealand for someone else at the age of 28.

Three years after joining a construction business back in Australia I was offered the opportunity to purchase a 10% shareholding. A few years later at 36 I bought out the founding director and became the managing director and major shareholder of what was then a $34M construction business.

We transformed that construction contractor into a $100M+ business over four years without any external capital, employing over 100 staff and exceeding all benchmark financial metrics. We then transacted this SME into a $250M joint-venture 'side business' with a subsidiary of one of the world's largest construction companies.

A MIND SHIFT TO EXPONENTIAL

What my experiences have taught me is that you must really consider a *first-mover* mindset, a willingness to determine what your tomorrow will look like. To not be a passenger in this fast-paced and highly competitive environment, but to grab the wheel as much as you can.

You may be a business leader, an aspiring manager, or even a business management student who wants to see, think, plan and act differently, but you don't know how to activate that point of difference. Or perhaps you are deep in the downside, looking for some different *thinking* and *doing* that will enable you to stand and fight, something that will deactivate your organisation's inertia and really start to move the needle.

As the COVID-19 health pandemic accelerates our freefall into global recession, you may be looking for a different kind of thought partnership to enable you to not only navigate this crisis, but to also enable you to come out the other side organisationally leaner, strategically smarter and competitively sharper.

Change is activated by what you say and what you do. It is enabled by different thinking.

If you are a leader looking for something to unleash your growth mindset, or simply an ambitious person wanting to create your own picture of what success could look like for you, *Stop the Bleeding* represents a mind shift from incremental management thinking to exponential business leadership, described through firsthand experience and success. Where do we truly learn how to manage and succeed in a troubled and declining market? Where is the textbook that specifically lays out strategies to optimise and maximise volatility, uncertainty, complexity and ambiguity? As a business leader with your back to the wall, how will you stop the bleeding in your business? How will you get to your *next*?

In this book I will show you how to optimise and maximise your people and your business.

A WILLINGNESS TO FIGHT BACK

Stop the Bleeding originated out of sleeves-rolled-up, down-in-the-trenches frontline executive-level leadership that navigated the fallout from the 2008 Global Financial Crisis, a period a few years after the crisis when cashflow caught up with most, when contracts were terminated and the construction pipeline dried up, when the supply chain melted, and default obligations were mounting. This is when banks rewrote the definition of risk.

Over a period of six weeks, having gone from hero to zero and staring down the barrel of an unforeseen insolvency, an aggressive and ultimately successful one-million-dollars-per-month turnaround became the foundation for this book. *Stop the Bleeding* digs deep into this period when every conceivable economic and business problem impacted all of us and created life-defining experiences.

This book promotes an alternative perspective around enabling people with an *outside-in* view of what success needs to look like. Based on an ability to think differently in a crisis, a willingness to stand and fight, a realisation that people are your ultimate enablers and an opportunistic mindset that extracts upside from downside, it is through sharing these experiences that you will start to see, think, plan and act differently.

Stop the Bleeding will subtly criticise traditional management practices. It offers simple models to reset often delusional thinking. It promotes the concept of co-creating people-enabled success, and of generating opportunity out of risk rather than allowing it to take you down. Fundamentally, it is also about being frontline, hands-on and hands-in.

Each chapter is set up as a chronological mind shift through business transformation.

We go back to the basics of people, leadership and strategy, and step through the cognitive process that surrounds business transformation. From the perspective of managing risk, we step from one situation to the next through deep insights designed to stimulate your growth mindset. I provide you with some of my frameworks and models, case studies and learnings. And I (now!) comfortably and cathartically expose myself through sharing my personal journey through this turbulent period in my business life. It was confronting to do so, however if you pick up just one different thought, idea or action that makes a difference, personally or organisationally, I have achieved my why and it was worth the effort.

Through sharing these extraordinary business circumstances and responses, you will see that it will only be through a journey of different *thinking* that you will unlock your ability for different *doing*. This book is not about construction businesses. It is about creating a compelling reason for *being in business*, it is about authentic leadership of people, it is about being adaptable in an environment of extreme disruption, and it is about balancing risk and opportunity. It could be any business.

ONE

GETTING TO *NEXT*

THE ONLY REASON TO LOOK BACKWARDS IS TO LEARN

In any business intervention – whether it be crisis management, product development or, say, a process improvement project – to clearly articulate what success needs to look like by when, you need to draw a line in the sand. A *that was then, and this is now, or next*, kind of approach.

To provide context around the mind shift I have learnt that enabled me to stop the bleeding in my business, this chapter is about *my what* and *my how* from a personal perspective. I go deep in places, and I am willing to do so because not only did I learn plenty from these experiences, I hope you might stretch your thinking also.

If necessity is the mother of invention, economic volatility, global political uncertainty and technological acceleration are the fathers of reinvention. I have drawn a line in the sand a few times, and I am sure I will do so a few more times before I am done.

I am grateful for being born with DNA that has enabled a decent work ethic. It instilled in me the interdependency of effort and outcome, the notion of ambition and personal improvement, and drew me in to the concept of risk and reward.

Work ethic created my first 'official' business as a subcontract carpenter at 22, building house frames with my brother Mark and some small commercial projects around Melbourne for another guy. I was working out of the back of my 1971 white Ford XW station wagon – affectionately known as the White Rhino – with my first direct report, Chloe the Blue Heeler.

My time on the tools lasted five years, and included my first business partnership, a six-month period with my ex-builder grandfather Jack Stone, renovating farmhouses in country Victoria. He threw me a lifeline when the world was unravelling at this time, through the 1987 stock market crash and the 1990 recession that Australia 'had to have'.

The aftershock of this period was still being felt a few years later, and I knew it was likely that I could soon be out of work. So I made the first move.

In a situation reminiscent of the welfare queues we see in the media today due to the COVID-19 pandemic and resulting economic crisis, I found my next opportunity on the jobs board at Centrelink. What is interesting about reflecting on this now is that it was my career sliding-doors moment – the period when I stumbled upon reinventing myself – occurring amid global economic distress not dissimilar to the recession the world is experiencing today.

The short story from there – that I will explain in more detail later – is that the desire to avoid becoming a recession statistic actually became my burning platform, enabling me to shift from building houses to managing 400 construction workers at the age of 25, and then to managing the overseas expansion of this same business at 28. Upon returning home, project and general management opportunities opened up for me at construction business APM Group, an SME that I eventually became managing director and a major shareholder of in 2004.

There may have been some entrepreneurial capability coming out that was developing at high school a few years prior. Through enterprises such as cigarette distribution, special price bookmaking and an identity management business I guess I was always finding a way to get to whatever I thought my *next* was going to be!

These experiences have motivated a desire for continuous learning and built the platform from which I now advise domestic and global corporations in optimising new businesses or transforming existing ones.

To me, work ethic is not 'entirely' working your fingers to the bone. It was always about the relationship between effort (working your fingers to the bone) and opportunity (getting to what and wherever was *next*). While work ethic introduced me to a privileged position of people leadership, business management and ownership, it also derived the purest definition of risk and reward. It also brought with it some pretty dark times in terms of business recovery and personal livelihood.

LEARNING HOW TO LEAD

At APM we exemplified a 'work hard and play hard' culture. It was something I willingly took responsibility for when I stepped into the big chair in 2004. Friday night drinks at The Water Rat in South Melbourne, lunch at Becco a few times a week, and numerous project completion celebrations at some of Melbourne's finest restaurants.

I loved being part of what I saw as an engaging and collaborative culture, and this is what I thought people and performance management was all about. Reward for effort was financial. There was nothing more to it.

I loved the reward this represented, and thought – as immature as that now seems – that it defined our success at the time. However, on the flipside, when our backs were to the wall, I have no doubt this resilience, hard work and collaborative mindset helped us knock down that very same wall more than once.

There was a period in the early 2000s when APM was known to operate as a revolving door – if you didn't cut it you were out, or if you felt you may not cut it you would jump first. Other than stepping up to larger and more complex projects, performance management and professional development were not specific disciplines. Without wanting to sound controversial, almost 20 years ago in an alpha-male-dominated industry and successful business, that was not unusual. It was my way or the highway, and I admit that I picked up that baton in 2004 and ran with it.

For a while anyway.

As the leader of the business, the productivity disruptions, the financial cost and the culture distraction of the revolving door was building an awareness in me. Moreover, it was starting to worry me. I was learning that consistency and capability in the people space needed to precede any serious growth strategies we had in mind. No people, no show!

After two years in the managing director's chair and as part of a strategy to corporatise the APM business, alongside an external audit, a technology roll out and an integrated management system, with additional internal and external support we embarked upon an initiative to enhance both our people capability and our people leadership ability.

As a group of construction guys, we didn't know what we didn't know, and so we needed to draw a line in the sand. And the only way we could do that was to profile our own leadership styles and that of the organisation as a whole, with the help of a consultant.

This was going to be great – I always enjoyed the competitive mindset of performance and score, and I was reasonably sure that as the ultimate leader of the business I would come out on top ... even though I didn't really know a thing about it. Delusional I know!

OFF THE CHARTS

At my follow-up personal feedback session I was shocked to receive a formal health warning brought about entirely because my 'red' perfectionistic and competitive behaviours were off the charts. They were literally drawn off the circumplex that was used to demonstrate the score I was so keen to receive. In my (weak) defence I can disclose that my 'blue' humanistic and affiliative behaviours were appropriate, yet I needed to consider developing some entry-level 'green' passive and dependent behaviours. Obviously, this consultant didn't know anything about the cut and thrust of construction, and I proceeded to explain to him that there was nothing to worry about.

Needless to say, I embraced the competition I had now created within myself to even up the circumplex.

It has been quite an awakening, to say the least.

From a mindset perspective I had been fixed firmly on effort and outcome – this constant treadmill of productivity at all costs was my narrow view as to the originator of success. When economies are thriving and there is plenty for everyone you can actually get away with this. It wasn't until we were weeks away from potential insolvency that the light went on for me that people, not processes, are our ultimate enablers.

When deep inside this period that quickly transformed from uncertainty to crisis in 2011, leadership and intervention became personal in both touchpoints with others and impact on livelihoods. And while I was grateful for a resilient and seemingly bulletproof leadership team, the buck stopped with me.

All feedback then and now says we had built by this stage a really positive culture around information and inclusion, and we had staff turnover down to 15% from 33%. Everyone knew where the business was headed, the part they each played in it, and what success could look like for them. Communicating that we were 'battening down the hatches' was a different version of regular information strategies; turning that volume up to now direct strategies around 'stopping the bleeding' was a fundamental and concerning shift.

Individual conversations led by staff around their personal circumstances, their mortgage risk and sustaining their livelihood generally kept replaying in my mind, day and night. I knew that as directors and shareholders, personally we were at the front of the queue for the worst possible outcome should it ever come to that, however I had a responsibility to more than a hundred staff and their families at the time. In my mind it was actually closer to four hundred people that were relying on me to get us through this.

Through a progressive six-month 'no surprises' strategy, we outplaced 39 staff to other businesses and people I knew, managed longer term exits with 18 others, and transacted only one redundancy. Removing almost 50% of our loyal staff was one of the hardest things I had to do at this time, however not only was their livelihood risk removed at that time, it created at very minimal cost the lean overhead structure that the business needed.

While work ethic was my predominant enabler – and to an extent, it still is – it took me a long time to learn there are other attributes which originate and centre around people that are the foundation for enduring success. I am proud to say I didn't get to today without evening up the red, blue and green behaviours over time. It remains a focus of mine.

Drawing a line in the people-leadership sand way back then made enabling people through business distress in the future somewhat easier. Though perhaps 'easier' is the wrong word. It helped me understand how my leadership impacts people, and how I could best enable them.

IF YOU DON'T ASK, YOU DON'T GET

Coming off the back of 50% revenue and profit growth the initial two years leading APM, I became interested in the opportunities that the Middle East was supposedly offering – negotiated projects, 20% margins and an almost infinite pipeline.

After numerous trips in 2007 to Dubai, Abu Dhabi and Qatar, I uncovered two real opportunities that would enable APM to align with global-scale contractors and accelerate our people, project and financial capability. As a low-risk entry, we were to provide staff initially and manage specific packages of works.

I was aware of the downturn in the US housing market as it had been happening since 2007, and while a couple of their second-tier lenders had filed for bankruptcy, I was relatively ignorant of world events. But when our potential Middle East partners withdrew interest almost overnight, I started to pay attention.

Fortunately for us, our global expansion didn't get off the ground. Although our initial strategy was to deploy people rather than invest capital, we still dodged a bullet.

Over the four years to 2008 and through exceeding 30% year-on-year growth (without any external capital or shareholder equity), transforming the APM business through tripling revenue, more than doubling the amount of profit, growing retained earnings 8× and net cashflows 10× was one of my most rewarding periods in business.

By the time the GFC hit Australia a year later we had just come off a record year. We were debt free and had the financial capacity to pursue numerous strategies if we needed to. However, the speed and scale of decline I had witnessed in the Middle East had me worried.

I remained fixed in my view that we had the capability and resources to continue to grow regardless of global economic uncertainty, however this was going to hit a financial capability ceiling. If we could leverage our recent period of sustained success and partner with one of the 'big guys', we could offer a substantial balance sheet and broader project capability in what was sure to be an intensely competitive period.

We aligned with PricewaterhouseCoopers and, following a search process throughout Australia, we executed a joint venture with Broad Constructions, a subsidiary of one of the largest contracting companies in the world, Leighton Contractors (now CPB and in turn, CIMIC Group). The coincidental thing about this deal is that Leighton Contractors was one of the opportunities that presented for us in the Middle East in 2007.

At the time, Broad's turnover was $400M across business units in Western Australia, Queensland and New South Wales, and Leighton Contractors' revenue was $4.5B globally. APM's turnover that year was $100M. We were happy to hang on.

This was an extraordinary deal and became a successful relationship. APM continued as a standalone business in our traditional market, and in addition we amplified our project and people capability via the joint venture while removing liabilities around project securities and working capital. The JV provided us a perfect world of unencumbered growth and quarterly profit distribution.

Our compelling story was now that we were a successful tier 3 contractor with tier 1 people and financial capability, contracting across a broader market and able to secure greater market share in a highly distressed and competitive economy.

We had drawn a line in the sand. It was game on.

FROM HERO TO ALMOST ZERO

We had just secured our first JV project, of which APM's 'slice' amounted to 60% of what was usually our forecast annual profit through fifteen smaller projects. Bankruptcy, bail-outs and stimulus packages were daily rhetoric. The Global Financial Crisis was really starting to run deep and wide.

We were still operating APM as a standalone business. That was one of the great things about the terms of our joint venture, however a major project outside of the JV didn't get off the ground. Then another two other institutional projects were delayed, putting a hole in APM's forecasts that year, adding financial pressure to our already 'at capacity' overheads.

Chasing work, taking the knife to margins and managing cashflow became business as usual inside APM, as with many others at the time. It was hardly the compelling story we had started the year with. We had become so invested in pursuing cashflow and building a warchest of cash reserves that we had secured a significant volume of projects and just couldn't wind back operations. We had 12 concurrent projects at the time.

We were constantly dealing with risk. We had forgotten what opportunity looked like.

It was a highly aggressive period, and we accepted the breakeven result that year only because our retained earnings account and reputation remained intact. And also, because the separate JV was successful in generating one large project return every quarter for almost two years. Although the APM business was now simply holding on, the JV remained a competitive proposition in the next project tier. We were APM with a different label, and that was compelling from our potential clients' perspective.

Post-Christmas, 2011 unloaded on APM even further. The proverbial music had stopped down in tier 3. The pipeline had dried up, competition had intensified, and the supply chain became even more unreliable. After a number of subcontractor insolvencies, our project step-in obligations (by virtue of their default) went from $600k to $4.5M over a six-week period. We had $5.4M in cash reserves, and overheads were draining $400k per month just to stay in the game. It wasn't going to add up.

We suddenly had six projects in distress. We posted our first ever loss that year. It was $5M.

It is interesting to reflect upon whether our perception of monetary value has changed over time? I recall a conversation with a potential turnaround client earlier this year where they were clear in their instruction to me that they weren't "committing energy" to the $1M problem, they were only focused on the other $7M problem. (I couldn't commit to solving part of a problem so I politely declined!) Whilst a number in isolation, the consequence 'scale' of our $5M loss in the construction industry today might be questionable however the impact of any loss with the word *million* attached to it is significantly painful at any time, in my opinion.

Our partnership strategy, the joint-venture lifeline that propped up the APM business both financially and reputationally, was my success. Being ignorant to the declining APM market and attempting to scale our core business rather than meeting an altered market was my failure.

Our APM turnaround strategy needed to be specific, high impact, without delay, and led by me in every direction. This is how we were to authentically prove how important it was, and what success was going to look like, by when. It was our best shot at receiving equally authentic buy-in in return.

All of the strategies we deployed are set out in more detail in the following chapters, however the upshot was we were leaner, we were responding to a different market, we were securing projects sustainably, we were retaining profits and forecasting positive cashflows. Our target was $1M upside per month over six months to get our head above water. Eventually we delivered a $7M turn-around inside nine months, returning the business to a $2M profit by year end.

But we weren't quite in the clear just yet. Having cleaned out our retained earnings account and with our head only just above water, we really needed a line of credit as back up to enable us to pursue appropriate growth.

Not surprisingly – and irrespective of our historical nil debt and a successful turnaround – banks weren't prepared to advance any facilities to a construction business, let alone one that was coming off a not insignificant loss. Fair enough. In fact, having the discussion with the banks was a mistake, opening the door to even deeper scrutiny around our ability to maintain project security facilities.

Our JV relationship was two years young and it was strong at both a personal and an organisational level, and I knew that as before, our previous performance as a joint-venture partner coupled with our turnaround success would need to be our leverage for whatever *next* was going to be.

While the JV was a sustainable and successful proposition continuing to collect those one-off larger project returns, it was the heavier financial encumbrances that were needed to rebuild APM as a sustainable standalone proposition – the cash reserves to prop up a bank guarantee facility in addition to working and growth capital – that were consuming my strategic thinking.

For APM there was potentially a more profitable business model with a diverse capability and sharing – or even offloading – of these financial covenants, but I wasn't sure that Broad or Leightons would go for it. Fortunately, the Broad Managing Director with whom I shared a great professional and personal relationship saw an opportunity to capitalise on its national expansion strategy by acquiring APM to wrap up Victoria and, in addition, take it across the border to South Australia.

We were quickly on the same page and negotiated a cash deal whereby Broad would acquire a majority stake in APM for in excess of $8M. This was an exceptional deal coming off a $5M loss the previous financial year, currently returning 3% on $70M, and with future maintainable earnings little more than a crystal ball exercise.

This acquisition would slot into their expansion strategy, escalating myself to the national CEO role providing succession to a planned exit for the Broad founder and managing director who was still a significant shareholder in the essentially Leighton controlled business. It would relieve APM of requiring project securities, remove the need for any banking relationship, and distribute capital to shareholders who hadn't received a dividend for 3 years, let alone a reasonable salary.

It was going to be an extraordinary, and quite an unbelievable, finish to the year, having gone from hero to almost zero, from loss to profit via an aggressive multi-million-dollar turnaround, while growing a JV as a side business.

It was a line in the sand that we had worked very hard for.

Within one month of agreeing terms and while waiting for Leighton to officially sign off, tragically the Broad Managing Director, my good friend Kari Rummukainen, died of a heart attack. Without Kari driving the potential acquisition and transition, Leighton understandably pulled the pin, and in fact a year later they terminated the joint venture completely, instead deciding to go it alone in Victoria.

We were down, but by no means out. I had been at war pretty much all throughout 2011. It was exhausting, but I wasn't going to surrender.

* * *

With the successful completion of the final two transformation and consolidation phases building a sustainable future for APM, I exited the business two years later, after 10 years as Managing Director and 16 years of extraordinary hands-on and hands-in experience through success and failure.

After all that, I now had a desire to go it alone and to solve problems for others.

LIVELIHOOD MAKES IT PERSONAL

I realised a couple of years later while trying to push some entrepreneurial thinking that I had retreated to a fixed mindset, that I had lost my risk mojo – or my opportunity drive – and, in fact, I realised I was still in survival mode.

Yet I didn't need to be, for any material reason. And I couldn't work out why I was.

I was doing what I set out to do after having left corporate life. I was managing risk and activating opportunity for others, using my recent turnaround, transformation and consolidation experiences to optimise and maximise whatever their *next* needed to be. I got a kick out of problem solving – in fact, that still remains my favourite thing. It was in this reflection that I had buried myself deep in well-paid and rewarding advisory work – activating a massive development pipeline for a global fund, creating an Asia-Pacific expansion strategy for an offshore technology business, travelling the world establishing a global procurement strategy for another, shutting down a loss-making construction business, negotiating multi-million-dollar dispute outcomes – that I realised I was still protecting our family livelihood.

I had worked hard for a long time, and it wasn't only individual goodwill that I was accumulating, it was also financial security. This was important both psychologically and materially to some-one who had started the entrepreneurial phase of their life dropping business cards in letterboxes by night, working out of the back of an old station wagon by day.

Some 20 years later my work ethic had retreated to a one-dimensional revenue-generating mindset, rather than being that enabler who got a kick out of creating opportunity. The entre-preneur was on extended leave, it seemed. With some external coaching, I found myself rewinding the clock a few years and acknowledging I was still in survival mode. I was like the soldier walking out of the jungle three years post-war believing there was still a battle to be won.

Looking back on the days at the height of the GFC, there were a number of threats from subcontractors seeking to escalate their payment as a priority or at least extract a personal guarantee that ensured imminent payment. Some of these I didn't worry about as experience told me some of the run-of-the-mill 'pay or else I know where you live' threats were at times par for the course in this industry.

Unfortunately, there were a couple of high-risk threats of poten-tial maximum consequence, so clearly described to me that I had to believe them to be real. Despite this, I had no alternative but to stick to my guns (no pun intended) and offer whatever the 30-, 60- or 90-day payment plan was that – at that point – was our only option. There was no point agreeing to something that we may only default on and possibly accentuate the likelihood and consequence of the threat.

While I have a fairly solid theory, I still to this day don't really know what the silent bikers' ultimate motivation was, however all of these various threats had escalated at a time when the industry and our business was at its highest risk of failure. My mindset was deep in family safety and business survival mode.

I don't claim to be a tough guy, and I'm pretty sure I'm not stupid – you do worry about this stuff. It took me a while to create some mental insulation around these thoughts. What helped was knowing that there was business stress everywhere and it was highly unlikely I was the only focus of their intimidation.

SH!T JUST GOT REAL

Around the 2011 *annus horribilis*, there was a five-year period of significantly reduced earnings personally via both remuneration and dividend. And fair enough, you might say. This is not a plea for sympathy. When you take on opportunity you are delusional should you decide not to accept nor acknowledge any likelihood of risk. We weren't working out of the back of a station wagon; we were the real deal. We were a $100M business that had maximised plenty of opportunities in the past.

And sh!t just got real. I was under no illusion. I got it.

As a business leader deep in the turnaround trenches, while stopping the bleeding among the daily operational grind and trying to 'keep the show on the road', I had numerous competing business objectives – I referred to this as my 'global strategy'. And also at risk was our personal livelihood and equally significant financial and personal commitments that underpin sustaining and surviving as a family of five – this was my 'domestic strategy'.

And if that is not a challenge in itself, here's the tricky bit: to ensure the success of our domestic strategy I needed to prioritise our global strategy.

When the project pipeline was diminishing, we left a multi-million-dollar dividend on the table to maintain the business's war chest. Eventually the business needed to spend all of it. The pending acquisition by Broad was going to plug this dividend gap and provide us cash flow relief. Until that deal was pulled.

Personal cash assets saw us through for a couple of years. To remove any future personal risk and distraction to the global strategy, and simply to provide a cash buffer, we offloaded the family house and set about a strategy of staying close to the market through buying and selling, or simply selling, property.

As a proud provider, selling the family home was a tough pill to swallow, and one that would have been so much tougher had I not had an amazing support base on the home front. Aggressive, timely and successful crisis management is not possible without having an unconditional 'live in a tent' partner, one who genuinely prioritises family, one who has succeeded at executive level in corporate life herself and who knows that at times you've just got to get sh!t done. Those who know my wife Mim will be nodding their heads in agreement, no doubt the strongest asset on my 'personal balance' sheet.

When livelihood gets personal, survival and protection is the predominant mindset, and it's an extremely difficult mindset to shift when the size of the prize (or problem) is so great.

FIGHT OR FLIGHT … AND FRIGHT

I still needed to work out where my risk mojo had gone so that I might be able to bring it back! Why was I completely focused on and enjoying managing risk for others, yet leaving my entrepreneurial opportunity parked in the back of my mind?

Bleeding one million dollars a month and understanding what corporate failure could look like, the aggressive multi-million-dollar turnaround that then followed, personally 'owning' the livelihood responsibility for hundreds of people, relentless daily financial negotiations at every level both internally and externally, not to mention the threatening environment … could possibly justify some emotional stress?

I resolved this thinking a long time ago. But what is the lasting cognitive impact, why did it take me a couple of years to really and truly move on?

Looking back now from a much clearer perspective and recognising how easily stress can occur, it is actually returning to the safe harbour of a fixed mindset that allowed it to happen. A watershed moment for me to say the least, but in the heat of battle for a very long time I refused to recognise that while advancing organisationally I was retreating personally.

I started doing some research and seeking advice.

Stress develops at speed, from an external event to an internal feeling, and then from a negative emotion to a physical reaction.

We are all familiar with the beginning and the end of this stress process, however where we let ourselves down is the inability, or lack of foresight or perhaps even the training, to intervene and redirect the steps in between. I know now that if we do not short circuit the internal feedback loop, we amplify the stressor. Bigger (perceived) problem creates a bigger (perceived) solution.

I don't suggest that 'dealing' with these internal disruptors is easy; in fact, I think that for the majority of us who successfully deal with stress we don't actually remove it, we survive it. And then, usually, we just move on. Others choose to remove themselves from it altogether. Good luck to them.

This dilemma is often referred to as the fight-or-flight response, a physiological response to a terrifying mental or physical event. The sympathetic nervous system stimulates the release of hormones that prepare your body to either stand and deliver or to run away to safety.

But I think there is another state of mind in this fight-or-flight spectrum, and that is fright, referred to in this context nowadays as 'freeze'. It is both an internal feeling and a physical reaction – it is a passive, almost paralysing, response as distinct from the escape via flight.

Neuroscience may say that fright is not a consideration in the flight-or-fight scenario, or that in fact it presents as freeze, how-ever on the spectrum of black to white I believe it is grey. I think I have proven that fight was a predominant mindset for me, however there was a period of time when the fight was over and I wasn't running away, that I was simply standing my ground and licking my wounds – 'in fright of' another fight?

Hmmm … there might have been something in that health warn-ing during the psychometric test feedback session back in 2006?

Despite all of these experiences, I can proudly say I have never looked backward, only forward – even with a bit of trepidation at times!

But deep insight into, rather than simply acceptance of, your envi-ronment and an awareness of mindset implications are easier said than done.

YOUR MINDSHIFT:
Don't look back

1. **Personal ambition.**
   The ability to build a clear picture as to how to get from the here and now, to your *next*. You don't need to kill it with analysis.

2. **People skills.**
   Authentic relationships and partnerships come from that two-way street where you constantly know who you can learn from and how you can add value in return. This is not about building social media 'connections'.

3. **Be an activist.**
   An ability to analyse, innovate, plan, delegate, manage time, solve problems and make decisions. To do whatever it takes.

4. **Accountable.**
   Hold yourself accountable, as this is where motivation will sustain, where the desired outcomes can be benchmarked, and where engagement by others can and will originate.

5. **Subtle mentors.**
   Surrounding yourself with great people is a no-brainer, however it is the commitment and resilience of your closest personal relationships and the brutal truth that they can offer that will serve as your ultimate motivation.

6. **Full disclosure.**
   It is okay to be concerned; not doing so is careless. Without sharing concerns and managing scenarios, they become worry and then panic. Survival mindset gets in the way of a growth mindset.

7. **Your arrival story.**
   Plan how you are going to walk through the front door at night; it needs to be different from how you left the office.

8. **Get real.**
   Money may not bring happiness, however it is an enabler, a pressure relief valve, a necessity. Say it, be real about it, and prioritise where and to what level it meaningfully adds personal value.

9. **Trust life.**
   Every cause and effect provides you an opportunity to respond. There is always an answer.

10. **Know what counts.**
    It's not about what you've got, it's about what you've got around you.

TWO

IT'S TIME TO MOVE ON

INGRAINED THINKING AND TRADITIONAL DOING GOT YOU TO WHERE YOU ARE TODAY

It used to be that businesses just needed to make money to survive, and to succeed. Nowadays businesses still need money to survive, however they need a whole lot more than that to succeed.

Business is like a game. It is a competition won or lost on the back of strategies to survive, played within a set of dynamic rules executed with varying levels of skill and experience by huge numbers of participants.

And this is the key to survival and success: among all of these participants, how will you truly differentiate yourself in this game?

Assuming you do have a product or service of value, and casting aside for a minute the well-worn textbook concept of unique value proposition, and the complication many people have in distinguishing their 'what' and their 'why', there are many fundamental components to this game. Here are the **10 tickets to the game of business** that you must co-create if you are to succeed:

1. **ACE people.** *Aligned*, *capable* and *engaged* willingness.

2. **A compelling story.** An external view of what success looks like.

3. **Opportunity.** Unique and distinctive markets.

4. **Capital.** Profit, cashflow and retained earnings. All three, all of the time.

5. **Adaptability.** Agile decision-making.

6. **Leadership.** A co-creator rather than dominator.

7. **Credibility.** Reputation through capability.

8. **Innovation**. A 'what if' mindset.

9. **Being data driven.** First-mover digital responses.

10. **A social conscience.** A desire to give back.

The following image illustrates the contradiction between divergent and convergent thinking and the chaotic and compelling business models that they create – two very different game plans.

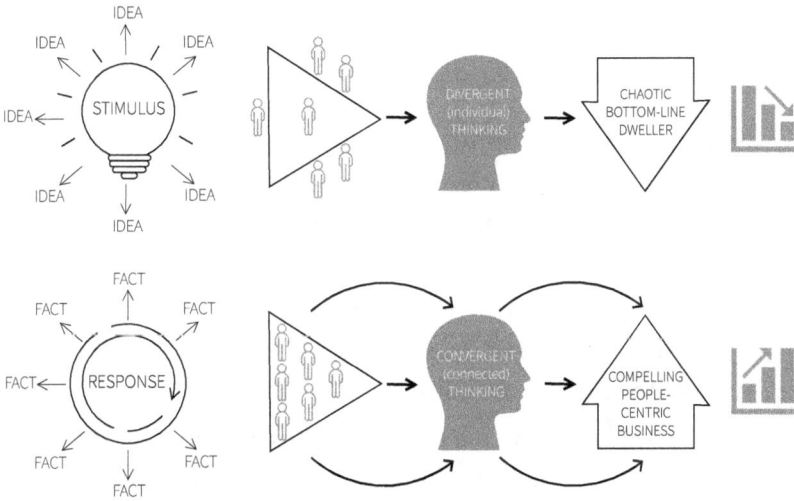

Figure 1. Opposing game plans

The necessity to survive and succeed is replacing at speed the traditional transactional and divergent hit-and-miss existence with a convergent, connected and compelling business model

* * *

In the following chapters we go deep into most of these 'tickets to the game', however to set the scene so you may start thinking and doing differently, I wanted to share my perspective on a few of the game-changers, those components or 'value adds' that are shifting traditional or mainstream business, and also where some of this fails.

HOLDING ON TO FAIL

Marc Stigter PhD suggests the way we still lead and organise our companies together with the way we strategically think and act is based on a 20th-century model. We are busy holding on to ingrained organising models unsuitable for managing today's complexities and opportunities.[1] We refer to this as *inside-out* thinking.

Here are **five characteristics of unsuccessful strategy** brought about by *inside-out* thinking:

1. Poor **strategic planning**:
    -   Strategy is simply a reactive process around conventional internal business metrics rather than data-driven external insights that create distinctive strategies.
    -   The plan is overwhelming as the goals and initiatives are too numerous to be able to prioritise critical actions and to allocate relevant accountability.
    -   The plan is based on a new version of an old strategy, and is likely tied to crude financial metrics around revenue and profit only.
    -   The strategic priorities are subject to excessive and constant change, there is considerable fatigue and no certainty in direction.

2. People without **capability**:
    -   Management teams are consumed with day-to-day operational responsibilities – representative of a bigger cultural problem around strategy disengagement – and they lose sight of the bigger picture.

---

1   Stigter, M. & Cooper, C. *Solving the Strategy Delusion*. 2015.

- Lack of leadership to the extent that not only is ownership of strategic outcomes unclear, there is no certainty around accountability and authority.
- Reluctance to have the difficult conversations and so empowering underperforming people to implement strategy at a level beyond the previous iteration that they were unsuccessful with.

3. Inefficient **organisational structures**:
    - A command-and-control leadership is deemed more appropriate to extract financial outcomes rather than engage-and-align to generate critical mass and enduring change.
    - The traditional flat structures that dominated your current predicament remain unchanged and are deemed appropriate to reinvent your business model in a fundamentally different environment.
    - There is no recognition of the organisational model required to manage and get in front of today's volatility, uncertainty and complexity, exacerbated by cumbersome levels of bureaucracy disguised as governance.
    - Apart from the Strategy Leadership Team, no-one knows what you are doing and thus there is no alignment, creating a push–pull effect.

4. Irrelevant **business models**:
    - There is an overdependence on a single customer and/or product revenue stream with little or no willingness for innovation.
    - Decisions are not customer-centric, they are made on the basis of your needs rather than customer behaviours and expectations.

- Going after all the business you can get as revenue and profit are worshipped as the measure of transformation success, rather than sustainable cashflows, productivity metrics and innovation adding value, for example.
- As long as we aren't going backwards it's a win.

5. **Complacency** and **delusion**:

- Transformation is simply a cost-cutting exercise as opposed to adding value through optimising fixed costs, extracting overhead synergies, seeking supply chain efficiencies, renegotiating commercial terms, and investing in new markets, to name a few.
- Delusional leadership: 'I can do this myself. Things will change. It's just a cycle. The people will stick around. We've done it without technology before. Cut the margins and we'll get it out of the supply chain ... '

You will note the common theme here is that if you are doing more of the same you are destined to fail. And if you are slow to move or you don't have your finger on the pulse daily, weekly and monthly, you will remain destined to fail.

Aligned with the first-mover principle, you really only have one chance to truly optimise and maximise any intervention.

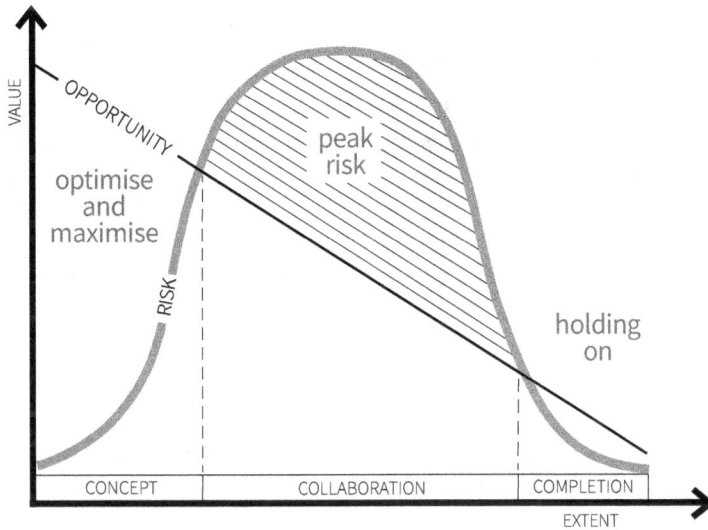

Figure 2. Risk and opportunity
*You really only get one chance to optimise and maximise –
it is never at the end*

FIRST-MOVER MINDSET

Change is the new normal, and it will never be this slow again. If the rate of change on the outside exceeds the rate of change on the inside, the end is near.[2]

In a business context the definition of innovation takes on an amplified digital connotation, bringing with it construed imperatives fundamental to business survival. It is becoming increasingly evident that the pace of change today is outstripping our ability to learn, with the recent environment of disruption, technology, automation and exponential change being labelled the 'Fourth Industrial Revolution'.

---

2   Welch, J. *Winning.* 2005.

But don't panic. Innovation is simply doing things differently to adapt to a changing environment. As a leader it should be part of your DNA to adapt, or as an emerging leader it should be high on your list of capabilities to learn. It is not entirely new learning. Try simplifying it to enabling a mindset of different seeing, thinking, planning and acting, every day.

The challenge for businesses however is that as the pace of change is so rapid, the people-led and (usually) technology-driven response needs to be equally as rapid. Traditional techniques and tools won't accommodate this acceleration.

In saying that, even the concept of agile is being innovated further to that of 'design thinking', a fast-tracked visualisation of user experience and a continuum of testing, feedback and learning. This is a concept represented in the following figure, and one that will innovate your origination steps 1 to 3 in our MindShift Method in chapter 9.

Regardless of the current *how*, the concept of change remains as relevant now as ever, and the exponential difference required is an ability to introduce real time – and sometimes even urgent – response or innovation.

But beware the downside, or perhaps the innovation anxiety tipping the scales too far one way. There is so much change going on in some organisations that management often overlook evaluating the impact of the latest change before initiating the next, increasing the likelihood of workforce disengagement, productivity paralysis and failed innovation.

Innovation is a long game of continuous improvement. Don't let it consume you to the point of going backwards, and eventually, of going nowhere.

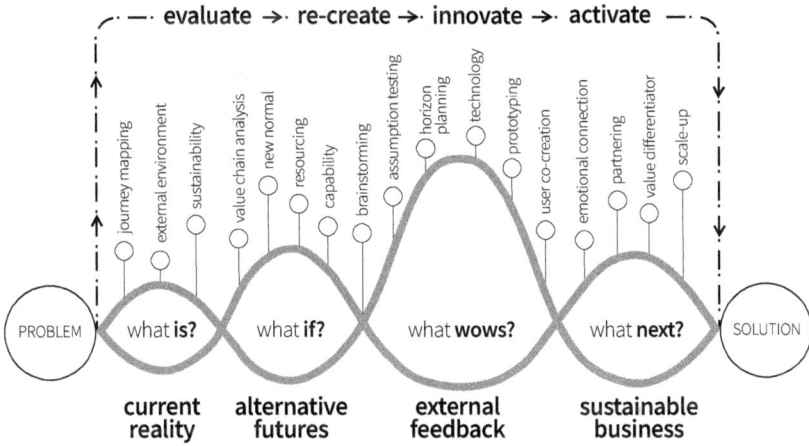

Figure 3. Innovative thinking

An outside-in *mindset that demands different seeing, thinking, planning and acting will create superior solutions addressing a future need. It is simply what next, at speed*

DESIGNED THINKING

There are some non-traditional but increasingly popular methods of thinking that are successful in moving the organisational needle. And they are gaining real traction.

Traditionally we are *inside-out* thinkers, meaning we start with an issue as we see it and consider solutions within that paradigm. This focuses on internal processes, systems, tools and products based on internal bottom-line thinking. From a business point of view the shareholders' needs and perspectives play a part in this type of thinking; a customer perspective is not usually taken into consideration.

By contrast, *outside-in* thinking is the ability to view an issue from multiple perspectives, and least of all your own. This means you look at your business from the customer's perspective and subsequently design processes, tools and products and make decisions based on what's best for the customer and what meets the customer's needs.

From a business point of view, having an open mind or an *outside-in* perspective enables us to anticipate and react to game-changing shifts.

To be an authentic *outside-in* thinker you may need to reassess your mindset and:

- accept that you do not have all the angles covered, and never will

- encourage new insights from whoever can offer them

- tolerate well-intentioned failures – fail fast, learn and move on.

Taking *outside-in* thinking to the next level is the relatively recent concept of 'design thinking', often described as a social technology or ethnography (a scientific description of people's habits), with people – and user-driven data – being the ultimate enablers. It is customer viewpoint amplified 10×.

From the perspective of creating innovative strategies, 'it usually describes processes, methods, and tools for creating human-centred products, services, solutions, and experiences'.[3] It is a sensing process that dilutes bias. It provides a deeper understanding of, say, a user's physical conditions, their business situation and the way they use and need a product, which builds

---

3   Bason, C. and Austin, R. 'The Right Way to Lead Design Thinking'. *Harvard Business Review*. Online. April 2019.

a close connection with the user way beyond one-dimensional online reviews and sales data.

A successful process must be experiential and is based predominantly on user-centric immersion, visualisation and innovation. Design thinking is not only a collaborative and iterative concept, it is a process that is a progressive experimental journey, best optimised when implemented and led by experienced practitioners.

It captures and creates uncontaminated visual assets along the way, the objective being to leverage human creativity and counteract human bias. It is another successful MindShift method for gaining deep insights in originating and activating strategic planning that we discuss in chapter 9.

From a generic perspective we can capture this undulation through divergent and convergent thinking described in figure 1, through the following four phases and nine progressive design thinking activities.

And just a reminder that it's pointless simply jumping on board with this different way of thinking and doing without understanding (1) what you are changing, (2) why you are changing and (3) with whom you are changing it.

PHASE 1: Customer Discovery – Recreate a meaningful user journey

Step 1   **Immersion.** Removing biases and identifying hidden needs by empathising with the user experience.

Step 2   **Context.** Understanding the context of the problem from the people perspective.

PHASE 2: Creative Alignment – Specific solutions that inform design criteria

Step 3   **Sense-making.** Avoid an immersion bias of seeing only what you want to see by challenging one another's individual perceptions.

Step 4   **Alignment.** Collaborative and creative discussions to agree on what is possible without the constraints imposed by the status quo.

PHASE 3: Emergence – Prototyping far-from-complete products and ideas

Step 5   **Ideate.** Individual brainstorming to produce creative ideas rather than negotiating compromises for best fit.

Step 6   **Pre-experience.** Prototype low-cost components that capture essential features. Incompleteness invites interaction and further innovation.

PHASE 4: Learning In Action – Releasing innovation expecting further refinement

Step 7   **Articulation.** Through feedback, test the implicit assumptions of each of the competing ideas previously prototyped.

Step 8   **Launch.** More advanced testing to identify improvement of the idea. User experimentation will reduces a person's fear of change.

Step 9   **Implement.** Done is better than perfect. Use launch to learn from and refine the best idea.

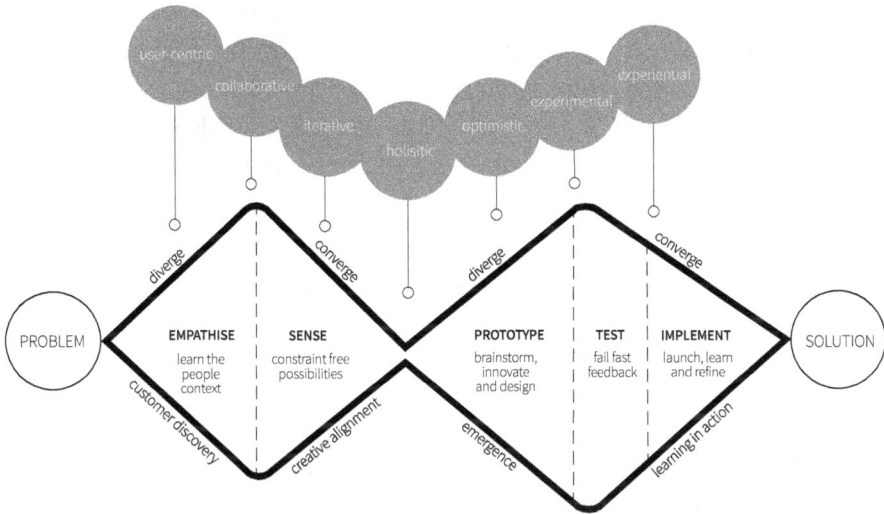

Figure 4. Design Thinking

Through immersing in customer experience producing data, transformed into deep insights, guiding teams to design criteria that they will use to co-create solutions

GET YOUR HEAD IN THE CLOUD

Digital disruption is driving major changes in how businesses design and execute strategy. It is important we understand that we are not necessarily creating new business with digital strategy, however we are willingly embarking upon a strategy that will reinvent our business, our offering and our skills. It is fundamental change.

And bring it on. Not only does digitalisation provide an opportunity for us to 'hang on' (sometimes just by our fingernails!) in the current environment of business acceleration, it also allows us to be at ground zero of this next 'Industrial Revolution'.

Disruption is another one of these management buzzwords we contend with on a daily basis, brought about by significant scale opportunities and threats created by powerful digital technologies. The cloud now conveniently and inexpensively delivers incredible processing power and digital storage, while inexpensive bandwidth and multifunctional personal devices make digital a constant part of modern life. The possibilities for new products, services, talent and business models is substantially impacting every sector of the economy.

For most of us, building and implementing digital strategy is unlikely to have been our core competency nor our fundamental revenue generator, however now more than ever there is substantial evidence of technology implementation driving financial outperformance, particularly if you are prepared to be a first-mover or very-fast-first-follower.

Similar to our discussion on innovation, your digital strategy response quite simply is relative to the scale of reinvention your business needs, and how deep your pockets are. Are you all in, or are you a toe-in-the-water kind of respondent? Are you a pioneer, a partner, or a passenger?

As the pace of digital-related change continues to accelerate, companies are required to make larger bets and to reallocate capital and people more quickly. These tactical changes to the creation, execution, and continuous modification of digital strategy enable companies to apply a fail-fast mentality and become better at both spotting emerging opportunities and cutting their losses in obsolete ones, which enables greater profitability and higher revenue growth.[4]

---

4   McKinsey Digital. 'A Winning Operating Model For Digital Strategy'. January 2019 survey.

Here are **nine perspectives that should inform your digital thinking**:

1. **Jump on.** Acknowledge and adapt to the digital-driven changes happening externally, as well as within. This business model innovation from an *outside-in* perspective will optimise first-mover or fast-follower opportunities.

2. **Integrate.** Initially new digital strategies will respond to a business model, however once implemented they should be then integrated as one strategy, creating a dynamic framework for continuous business transformation.

3. **Be tech savvy.** Businesses must educate their leaders on digital and encourage agile offensive thinking, producing insights that test, learn and correct quickly, rather than rigid defensive 'compliance' perspectives.

4. **No pain, no gain.** Be prepared to fail fast, cut your losses and move on.

5. **Build partnerships.** Rather than pioneering a digital solution alone, consider partnering with existing digital ecosystems. Strong digital platforms will enable new customers and marketplaces, broader industry boundaries, data sharing and learning, and the benefits of large-scale network effects.

6. **Create innovation clusters.** Hedge your bets. A mix of digital adjustments to existing products (bringing some revenue surety) as well as brand-new digital offerings is a strategy often deployed by early adopters.

7. **Go early.** Don't be afraid to invest in digital talent early. Technology is one thing, however qualified digital talent is a scarce commodity, as the pace of digital still outstrips the supply of people who can deliver it well.

8. **Mergers and acquisitions.** Consider a transaction to supersize the building of new digital capabilities rather than trying to build them through a slower, organic approach. (However, be aware that this can be a lengthy process, sometimes at odds with the concept of fast-paced digital-led innovation, especially during times of crisis.)

9. **Reset metrics.** Redefine how you measure success and move away from old metrics that are no longer meaningful indicators of economic success, such as market share, and value more productivity-type metrics, for example.

AUGMENTED HUMAN TALENT

The world is now well entrenched in the use of artificial intelligence (AI) and the process of machine learning (ML). The next level of business process improvement will use natural language processing (NLP) technologies to predict performance, enable optimisation and bring confidence to outcomes.

Technology is creating exponential data analyses that trigger predictive modelling, improve scenario management and unlock decision-making. The significance of this is it has enabled the deployment of augmented humanity (AH) to enhance human capability. The earliest innovations show that as humans we have always developed tools to augment work, however the AI technology now available to us has enabled the creation of an even more powerful capability.

Having automated routine cognitive work, technology has now entered the underdeveloped arena of non-routine cognitive work, where human analytical and problem-solving skills dominate. Within organisations, AI will disrupt nearly every role and function, while elevating the relationship between human and machine. It is only a matter of when, and to what magnitude.

Augmented talent is the human capability that can drive these technology outcomes. And taking it another step further, an augmented leader is one who has the capability to leverage technology to make fast, sophisticated, data-driven decisions that direct workers' activities in partnership networks, not through chains of command. For example, virtual meeting rooms (VMRs) and augmented reality (AR) allow teams to connect, interface and co-create simultaneously while removing geographical barriers. Some companies use virtual reality (VR) technologies to eliminate logistical problems in recruiting, reduce hiring bias and accelerating the process, as one example.

However, there are limitations to this whole concept of augmented human talent, whether it be the technology or the enabler, the people. For now, anyway.

The hardest activities to automate with currently available technologies are those that involve managing and developing people and the expertise for making decisions around creative work. AI and AH can enhance but will not replace human cognitive functions or emotional–social interaction.

Neither can AH replace (currently!) a leader's creativity, strengths, aspirations, values or ability to make sense of experiences. However, AI will augment those qualities and assist leaders to leverage them to make decisions that optimise business outcomes.

Technology has also both expanded and connected the freelance or 'gig' economy. As a freelancer there is no requirement to collaborate, to adopt a company culture, or to work to a schedule. Digital connectedness has created a whole new way of working.

But there is also escalated risk of isolation, ill health and income insecurity.

* * *

There is no doubt this future way of working will impact teams and the places within which they will co-exist, a future that will comprise employees, gig workers and machines operating side by side. The way teams interact virtually will affect organisational culture, values and alignment. Systems of accountability and development will have to adapt to this disjointed new reality.

Domestic businesses now forced to operate in a digital or virtual world have much to learn from those many successful global organisations that have been executing best practice remote team management for decades.

Adding to the complexity of business as usual, leaders will need to play a critical role in ensuring that augmentation and technology – and the physical separation this creates – does not erode the culture that underpins a business's collective purpose. Efforts to maintain relationships, effective two-way communication, critical thinking, co-operative decision-making, and developing competencies for example are now top of mind, brought about by the coronavirus pandemic.

These cognitive human attributes are the qualities that will help leaders achieve success. And as technology gets better, cheaper, faster and more accessible, the things humans can do that machines can't will only become more valuable.

As I write this, COVID-19 is disrupting the traditional way of living and working in the absence of a vaccine and with the necessity for physical distancing to flatten the curve. We have been forced into remote working, our children are online learning, we are attending family celebrations by video conference, and a doctor's appointment is now a tele-health conference. Lockdown has pushed nearly everything online around the world, and businesses are being forced into finding new ways to add immediate and low-cost value. Business as usual is now exponentially different.

Big technology firms, for example, are investing in personal prediction technology – the type of machine learning and artificial intelligence that online retailers use to 'push' that perfect set of golf clubs to your inbox – to inform strategies to mitigate the current and any future health crisis. Subject to building reservoirs of reliable data, they are analysing personal and community health information to forecast clinical risk and its impact on our health system.

Another example is the justice system whereby societal lockdown has shifted prisoner visitation online, not only removing virus contagion risk but also removing any risk of contraband entering facilities. Due to the ease at which the online visitation has been enabled, some facilities have increased the frequency of this virtual contact as a means to enhancing prisoner welfare. A gradual transition to virtual visits was apparently a longer term proposition, a five year plan, one that would have been controversial had it not have been for the disruption created by a global heath pandemic.

Have *you* considered where you to need to develop your skills to stay in front of, or at least up with, this exponential curve?

YOUR MINDSHIFT:
Don't be afraid of going first

1. **Co-create.**
   Collective thinking is the game changer, producing multiple perspectives that generate multiple and diverse opportunities.

2. **Skill fit.**
   Be clear on where you need to develop your skills to stay in front of, or at least up with, exponential growth.

3. **Tech savvy.**
   Part of this skill gap and skill fit acknowledgement is ensuring that a hierarchy of leadership is educated on digital. Don't leave it all up to just a few people.

4. **Growth mindset.**
   If we are to succeed in implementing enduring change we first need to unlock the biases and unwillingness to innovate that is entrenched in a fixed mindset.

5. **The new normal.**
   Embrace this new volatile, uncertain, complex and ambiguous world. It is not going away. A challenge ultimately provides the energy for truly making a difference.

6. *Outside-in.*
   From a business point of view, having a customer-centric perspective enables us to anticipate external variables and react to game-changing shifts.

7. **Design thinking.**
   An innovative, iterative and sensing process that dilutes bias and creates a deeper understanding of broader customer parameters, way beyond one-dimensional online reviews and sales data.

8. **Let go.**
   Unsuccessful strategy is brought about by holding on to ingrained management practices led by incapable people, inefficient organisational structures and irrelevant business models. Sorry, but it is.

9. **Data driven.**
   Superior data management and analytics are essential capabilities that support strategic decision-making and, ultimately, business performance optimisation.

10. **Big picture.**
    Agile businesses predict ahead of time *what's next*.

THREE

PREPARE YOUR GAME FACE

IT HAS EVERYTHING TO DO WITH HOW YOU SHOW UP

Leadership is a strategy in itself, an enabling strategy. A how. It is about co-creation not domination, and it originates with a mindset.

We are all leaders at varying degrees of influence. It is not a position nor a title, nor is it only the domain of the C-suite or other executive-level managers. At any level, a large part of your role and your success in it depends on your ability to influence people, opinions and outcomes. It is about crafting a message that resonates and communicating it effectively to inspire others to act.[1]

The concept of transformational leadership was introduced more than 40 years ago, and has been developed or modernised considerably since. It has evolved to that of visionary or responsive leadership, and it remains one of the most important concepts in business due to its adaptability, agility and willingness to leverage what is now, and always, a dynamic business environment.

A modern leader's success will gain momentum through:

- the ability to create a vision of what success looks like
- being a motivator of people, inspiring discretionary effort
- the capability and experience to manage the delivery of the vision
- being an effective team builder and a coach
- foresight to capitalise on changes in the business environment.

Amid such factors as globalisation and disruption fuelling this unrelenting pace of change the truly successful leaders are active, they are hands off, on and in, as and when required.

---

1   Naidu, Y. *Power Play: Game changing influence strategies for leaders.* 2016.

Perhaps the most simple visual for this innovative style is for us to consider that sitting behind a desk is a very dangerous place from which to lead a business. In fact, it is a thing of the past, an ingrained 20th-century management practice leading nowhere.

Hanging onto yesterday's outcome is irrelevant today. In this chapter we discover the frontline leadership mindsets and actions that make a difference, the innovative doing and thinking from which people are motivated and enabled to achieve success.

As a leader looking to extract discretionary effort from your people, it is all about how you 'show up'.

LEADING WITH MEANING AND PURPOSE

There is much contention around defining the most appropriate leadership style that aligns with today's complex business environment, however it is the very dynamic nature of this environment that ensures it is not a one-size-fits-all. Success will originate from a unique and complementary arrangement of numerous styles.

The **seven proactive leadership styles that enduringly make a difference**:

1. **A visionary leader.** Drives progress through change having earnt trust for new ideas and having inspired employees through previous success.

2. **An entrepreneurial leader.** A mindset to do more with less, focused on enduring success and excited about making the competition irrelevant.

3. **A coaching leader.** Recognises individual strengths, weaknesses and motivations; able to receive discretionary effort through developing this.

4. **A transformational leader.** The organisational version of the coach; has a bigger picture commitment to maximising an organisation's objectives.

5. **A responsive leader.** Able to quickly adapt to a changed environment and bring people along for the journey. Usually starting as a visionary leader.

6. **A participative leader.** An 'energetic' democratic leader who asks for creative input and feedback, optimising employee engagement and workplace satisfaction.

7. **A pacesetting leader.** Motivating fast-paced environments where people are already on board, enabling a 'go for it' performance-based collective mindset.

Making no apologies for ditching some of the outdated leadership styles that will not respond or adapt to dynamic environments, here are the types of leadership you should be leaving behind:

- **Transactional** – not creative; focused only on performance and reward; known to respond to failure with disciplinary action.

- **Bureaucratic** – inflexible and hierarchical; focused on rules and procedures.

- **Servant** – personal fulfillment becomes before commercial upside (great for a non-profit, however).

- **Autocratic** – authoritarian; focused almost entirely on results and efficiency and likely to make decisions without collaboration.

- **Laissez-faire** – hands off; focusing mostly on delegating and providing little or no supervision, potentially impacting motivation and output.

I am attempting to paint a clear picture that command-and-control leadership styles – the transactional, bureaucratic and autocratic behaviours – have perished under the heat of globalisation and innovation. As companies escalate efforts to collect, manage and respond to data, command-and-control leaders are at extreme risk of missing crucial perspectives if they don't find ways to bring more of their colleagues into important conversations.

Command-and-control, or 'yell and tell' as Yamini Naidu describes in her book *Power Play*, is a rigid hierarchy that promotes individual behaviours, produces conflict, and destroys innovation. It is an outdated, inside-out business model. (Command-and-control leadership *may* be effective in the case of extreme crisis management to 'stop the bleeding'.)

What is important about the above proactive leadership styles is that there is no one stand-out winner. Sure, let's see if we can dial in a visionary Chairperson, an entrepreneurial Chief Executive and a transformational Head of Finance, but we all know it doesn't quite work out that way. It is actually all about which style best optimises and maximises what is in front of them. And from a wider business perspective it's all about a mix of styles, the shared mindsets that lead to exponential thinking and exponential enterprises.

From a personal leadership–style perspective, we know we can change our mindset, and so we know we can change our leadership or management style.

Businesses adapt because people adapt.

HEAD, HEART AND GUTS

To be a leader in today's business environment, you need to use your head, demonstrate heart, and act with guts.[2] You need an ability to set strategy, to show empathy and to make decisions.

There is no doubt that when dealing with a crisis of any scale, keeping our thoughts and behaviours in check may be as difficult as dealing with the risk itself. All of a sudden we are dealing outside of business as usual, where change can be emotionally intense and combine with confusion, fear, anxiety, frustration and a feeling of helplessness.

And from a position of leadership, how do we deal with our people's reactions to organisational change, the rolling eyes, the 'here we go again', and 'haven't we tried this before' innuendo? How do you juggle this, knowing that for some people the experience of going through change can replicate grief or loss? Knowing also that change can be physically and emotionally draining, it often leads to burnout, and can escalate an even greater resistance to change? Not all people see, think and feel the same.

In crisis, turnaround, transformation – whatever the change extent – we need to display the behaviours that we need our group or team to emulate. We need to be adaptable rather than resistant, accepting rather than emotional, accountable rather than accusing, and positive rather than negative. In very simple terms, it is leading by example. Perhaps it is exemplar leading?

While the above behavioural traits will not satisfy the emotional intelligence academics, they do capture the four pillars of self-awareness, self-management, social awareness and relationship management.

---

2   Dotlich, D., Cairo, P. and Rhinesmith, S. *Head, Heart & Guts*. 2006.

The challenge in any organisational setting is that, in spite of the widespread use of the term 'emotional intelligence', how many of us really know what it is, and or can demonstrate it sustainably? I haven't nailed it, and cannot tell you that I practise it every day. I am human, after all.

However, after quite a bit of learning the hard way, I do know that it's not *just* about being empathetic or understanding someone else's point of view. And so, here are **10 things that emotionally intelligent people don't do**:

1. **They are not opposed to learning.** They are prepared to accept the advice of others, or have their beliefs challenged and not afraid of doing something differently.

2. **They don't just focus on self.** They have an ability to look at the world and its people from a bigger picture point of view, outside of their own needs and wants.

3. **They don't sweat the small stuff.** They have an ability to be resilient and agree to disagree, and a preparedness to learn from the past rather than dwell on it.

4. **Their reactions aren't reckless.** They have a calculated response rather than panic and fear, enabling appropriate stress management and better decision-making.

5. **They don't hold a grudge.** They have a focus on the solution rather than the problem, and make an effort not to get caught up in the reasons why not.

6. **They don't lose it.** They manage conflict successfully through good relationships and communication, and are able to convey thoughts in a respectful manner.

7. **They don't fake it.** They don't let things build up and are not emotionally dishonest. It is okay to tell it how it is from your perspective, respectfully.

8. **They don't act before thinking.** They have an awareness through assessing situations logically and with fact so that responses are measured and proactive.

9. **They don't lose sight.** They understand what is within their control, and what is not. It is pointless beating yourself up for things that you have no ability to influence.

10. **They don't embrace negativity.** They have an unwillingness to be dominated by fear or disappointment. You may need to accept it first, and then you can move on.

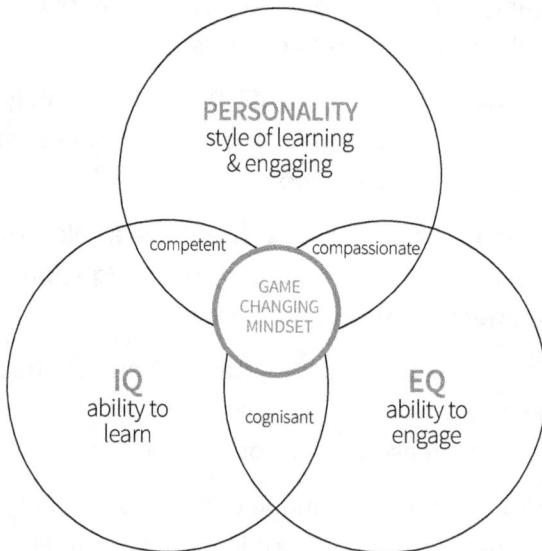

Figure 5. Demystifying emotional intelligence
*You need some of all three – not the sum of all three –
to leverage a game-changing mindset*

One of the challenges of emotional intelligence is that it's usually labelled as an individual competency, when the reality is that most work that is conducted inside organisations is done by a collaboration of people. From my experience, a business with a couple of emotionally intelligent people, or let's say people with appropriate leadership balance, will not guarantee an emotionally intelligent business.

To be most effective, the team needs to create emotionally intelligent norms – the attitudes and behaviours that eventually become habits – that support behaviours for building trust, group identity and group efficacy. The outcome is complete engagement in tasks.[3]

Groups will be most effective when collaboration is unconditional. People stop holding back when there is mutual trust and respectful interactions. Emotionally competent teams will have the capacity to face potentially difficult information and will actively seek constructive advice on the basis that these external opinions are the foundation of thinking and doing differently, or better.

SHOWING UP BELOW ZERO

Let's have a look at a very powerful example of great leadership and putting on your game face in extreme circumstances. Sir Ernest Henry Shackleton (1874–1922) was an Irishman who led three British expeditions to the Antarctic. He was sent home early for health reasons on the first, and didn't quite get to the South Pole on the second.

---

3   Druskat, V. and Wolff, S. 'Building the Emotional Intelligence of Groups'. *Harvard Business Review*. March 2001.

At almost the same time as the outbreak of WWI Shackleton set out on his third attempt. He set about raising capital and hiring a crew of 27 men to sail the ship *Endurance*.

Shackleton had learnt much about people on his previous two expeditions and hired the *Endurance* crew based on his assessment of attitude first, and then skill. Each man he hired had undertaken an interview with him where they were asked to sing a song, dance or recite poetry, skills far removed from naval competence. Shackleton felt that a willingness, or not, to participate in such a random interview task would allow him to get to their default character and provide him comfort that they have an ability to deal with whatever was thrown at them.

On this third expedition, within 80 miles of the Antarctic coast, disaster struck when the ship became locked in a vice of icebergs and was slowly crushed. As the ship sank, the crew escaped by setting up camp on the sea ice.

After three months floating around on the ice, his optimism for a rescue waning, Shackleton – 'The Boss' as he was known – believed that the expedition was over. Realising that the original goal was now unattainable, this is the point at which he pivoted from salvaging the original expedition to now focusing on survival and recovery.

Shackleton and his crew would be living in tents and upturned lifeboats, with diminished food supplies, floating on icebergs and with minimal daylight, for 20 months. His new worst-case scenarios could be mutiny, ice melt, anxiety, health, temperature and food. His ultimate challenge was now how to create stability, how to manage the energy of self and team, and build a consensus mindset of overcoming adversity as a team rather than individually.

It is well documented that Shackleton showed up every day as a leader. His body language was upright and his demeaner confident, not displaying his inner anxiety. He genuinely cared about his men and believed in rescue. In the 1930s in a BBC interview, many of the survivors were quoted as saying, 'The Boss made us each believe that we could do it.'

Shackleton knew that routine was important to enable team stability and a belief in self. He implemented a regime of 'mental medicine', insisting that everyone must walk three miles each day, that there was no retreating to tents after dinner, and that the random tasks they displayed at their dockside interview were to be the basis of evening activities.

He demonstrated and distributed empathy. If he noticed one man struggling, he would order up hot milk for the entire crew so that those struggling were not singled out. All of this was to sustain camaraderie.

Despite feeling guilt around not heeding a serious weather warning that was eventually responsible for their predicament, Shackleton didn't own it publicly as he had to keep the men's faith. And despite his reputation as a knighted explorer, survival became the greatest mission of his life. A mindset shift to 'owing it to these men' empowered him through moments of self-doubt and developed in him escalated resilience, improvisation and determination. It's remarkable the group didn't turn on him.

Maritime law at the time decreed that shipwreck removed any liability on Shackleton to pay his crew. He had, however, committed to paying them out of his own pocket on their return, and so had been able to maintain the crew's engagement as they held on to this 'silver lining'.

After drifting on the ice for almost two years, they saw an island, and after strapping three lifeboats together they landed on the inhospitable Elephant Island. Shackleton and five crew then departed again, and successfully navigated rough seas on an 800-mile voyage back to the South Georgia Whaling Station.

It was more than four months later when he returned to Elephant Island, and then returned to safe harbour in South America with all of his original 27 crew. It was almost three years from departure when the crew finally arrived back to the UK.

There is something incredibly powerful and sustaining about leaders who own their mistakes and yet keep facing forward and motivating us to achieve better and more difficult things as a group, as opposed to what we could ever achieve on our own. There is no doubt that succeeding in unlocking discretionary effort through a crisis is enabled initially by these **five resilient leadership behaviours**:

1. **Focus.** Being prepared to engage people with the right attitude and skill, not simply skill alone. Looking at the bigger picture of 'what if'.

2. **Compassion.** Connecting with each person individually and regularly, from both a personal and organisational perspective.

3. **Empathy.** Building authentic individual and group rapport creates a critical mass of momentum and a reservoir of goodwill.

4. **Messaging.** A combination of 'we can do this' and 'I've got your back' distributes subtle empowerment for mutual successes.

5. **Commitment.** Remaining present and accountable all the way through, and being a leader every single day.

Shackleton later travelled through the UK and US on the speaking circuit to settle his expedition debts. He returned to the UK, and after putting out a call to his previous crew, 12 of the 25 that remained travelled from around the globe to join him in 1921 on his fourth attempt at Antarctica. Unfortunately, he died of a heart attack during this expedition.

While Shackleton never achieved his life's ambition of getting to the South Pole, he was defined by who he became in a very turbulent situation, how he made himself better in dire circumstances, and how he affected other people positively throughout.

It is without doubt that great leaders are made, not born.

MANAGING THE SECOND ARROW

Navigating a business through any phase – whether it be expansion, transformation or crisis – is a powerful opportunity for personal growth. (Let's focus on the positives!)

From the perspective of crisis, our mental state often seems only to intensify an already challenging situation, becoming a significant obstruction in itself. In fact, we often don't even need to face a real crisis event or bad news for our minds to wander to the point of distraction and negative 'what if' thinking.

Resilience is about emotional strength. It's about your ability to adapt and bounce back when things are not going to plan. And the great thing about it is resilience is a skill you can learn. Learning from challenging experiences will allow you to move forward differently, and positively.

Individuals are very good at understanding linear trends and not so good at understanding events that come out of left field. We are wired to pay attention to uncertainty and threats, we can become anxious at alternatives, and at almost all costs we will attempt to influence outcomes. It is human nature. However, more often than not it's an inability to appropriately manage these behaviours that will lead us to making short-sighted decisions.

From an organisational perspective this behavioural cause and effect is considerably multiplied; the trick is learning how to make good decisions in these circumstances.

The best way to resist the call-to-action alarm bell is to 'cool the jets'. Slow down. Panic forces people into thinking they must act *immediately*, assuming this will quell the threat. Slowing down allows you time to deliberately reason with data and to carefully assess the situation to influence your decision-making. This is not to say that quick decisions are not appropriate, as in many crisis situations they will be, however be aware that many situations may also warrant inaction. It is also okay to say and do nothing, if that's what circumstances call for.

Your response will only be as good as your organisation's structure. Distributed leadership enabling collaboration and buy-in will be able to gauge whether quick actions will reduce organisational stress in the long term, rather than creating more problems than they solve.

From the perspective of crisis management, here are **10 resilience-building initiatives that will create a culture of confidence**:

1. **Stabilising.** Organisational stability provides people with a sense of confidence, security and optimism during any form of disruption, and will enable them to slow down and make effective decisions as the situation evolves.

2. **Enquiring.** Permit a culture of *why* and *why not*. Realising that it is very unusual for a cohort of people to all be on the same wavelength will allow you to not only receive different perspectives as a means of potential problem-solving, you

may get closer to what success needs to look like on the other side of this more quickly.

3. **Prioritising.** Focus on what matters most, and then what is critical in keeping the business running. This will dilute uncertainty and declutter decision-making. From a leadership perspective, the critical success factors to this are discipline and communication. Staying the course and (almost) over-communicating will build positive *thinking* momentum.

4. **Including.** This is really about being 'all in' with your people and not being selective about who needs to know what, a surefire barrier to performance which will undermine organisational stability and individual confidence. This also relates to working around existing systems and processes to enable connection among all employees.

5. **Learning.** Use success and failure experiences as learning moments. Through demonstrating an environment of safe conversation, focus on the 'what worked' and 'what didn't' dialogue rather than blaming and shaming. Consider documenting these as the foundation for new models for organising a new way of doing.

6. **Planning.** You will not succeed in building enduring resilience without having a plan for recovery. Even an indicative, dynamic, this-is-what-success-*could*-look-like kind of plan with a few contingencies will give your people something to look forward to, something they can align themselves to, and something they may be prepared to deploy discretionary effort for.

7. **Promoting.** Stability comes about through portraying confidence, strength and positivity. This does not mean denying reality or providing a false sense of hope; in fact,

acknowledging setbacks and moving forward is promoting optimism. What is the point of pessimism?

8. **Reassuring.** Do everything reasonably possible to alleviate people's fears by recognising their role in managing a crisis, the value they create in doing so, and their future from a capability and career perspective. Don't over-promise. You don't have to offer them a promotion or a reward, but acknowledging their worth allows them to look beyond 'the job'.

9. **Optimising.** It is not always possible to do more with less, however you must consider an overall picture of organisational wellbeing centred on workload and what you can do to relieve individual pressure. Exhausted, distracted and disengaged individuals will undermine organisational stability.

10. **Storytelling.** A purposeful, authentic story in business can influence, persuade and motivate people.[4] Those leaders who are prepared to put themselves out there sharing stories of success, failure and learning are truly leading with care and compassion. We will all go the extra mile for an authentic boss we can trust, right? This is the key to nurturing resilience.

There is no doubt that sh!t happens in business and personal life. It's all about how you deal with it. Or as Buddhist teachings say, *pain is inevitable, but suffering is optional.* I don't practice Buddhism, however I am an avid personal development reader. The concept of resilience reminds me of the 'second arrow'.

To paraphrase a Buddhist parable, Buddha once asked a student, 'If a person is struck by an arrow, is it painful?' The student said

---

4 Naidu, Y. *Story Mastery: How leaders supercharge results with business storytelling.* 2019.

yes. Buddha then asked, 'If the person is struck by a second arrow, is that even more painful?' The student said it was. Buddha then explained that, 'In life, we cannot always control the first arrow. However, the second arrow is our reaction to the first. And with the second arrow comes the possibility of choice.'[5]

From an individual perspective the first arrow is the trigger event, whatever it is that has caused the suffering. The second arrow is the one we self-inflict, the inward-facing blame game for why we are where we are.

From an organisational perspective, crisis is the first arrow. The one we don't see coming. (For example, as I write this, much of the world has gone into lockdown because of a virus nobody had even heard of just a few months ago.) Our emotional and psychological response to the crisis is our second arrow. The second arrow is also unavoidable, and in fact these reactions are quite simply human nature. We can, however, have some control over the second arrow, whereas we can have no control at all over the first. With an open-mindedness or an acknowledgement that with risk comes opportunity and that with a problem comes the solution, the damage caused by the second arrow can be managed, and the recovery process can be enabled.

The risk is that the uncertainty gets the attention, produces information, and forces a reaction. The opportunity is acknowledging we can control our response to the uncertainty.

GETTING THROUGH THE FOG

For a very long time I never really accepted the concept of stress. You work hard, you play hard, you push through and you get it

---

5 Burlingame, E.W. *Buddhist Parables Translated From the Original Pali,* 1922. Reproduced 2018.

done. At times you may need to wear full-body armour to aggressively and effectively defend, but whatever happens, you push on and you 'deal'. You back yourself.

Seriously? We all now know that's delusional thinking, including me.

It was only after a couple of years of trying to reignite an entrepreneurial mindset that I was able to acknowledge I had suffered from stress – psychological trauma, if you like – and probably to some extent even burnout, which is the physical effect when stress becomes excessive.

Picking up on my fight-or-flight, and fright, theory, I dug deep into the scientific foundation behind stress and came across this thing called 'cortisol' – the body's main stress hormone. With apologies to neuroscience again, the simple version of the stress response – within my business process analogy – is that the sympathetic nervous system sends an internal order to the adrenal glands to produce cortisol, the body's alarm system that deploys the main stress hormone, the quality and quantity of which is managed by the hypothalamus and pituitary glands in your brain which distribute via your blood.

If purchasing got the order right in the first place then you should have an appropriate quality and quantity of cortisol to distribute across your mood, motivation and fear; impacting blood sugars, blood pressure, food processing, sleep quality and energy levels. The following image shows how I 'processed' this concept.

With a very high-level view of the 'stress science' – according to me – I set out on a private campaign to learn more about the lasting impacts of stress so I could start formulating a strategy to knock it on the head.

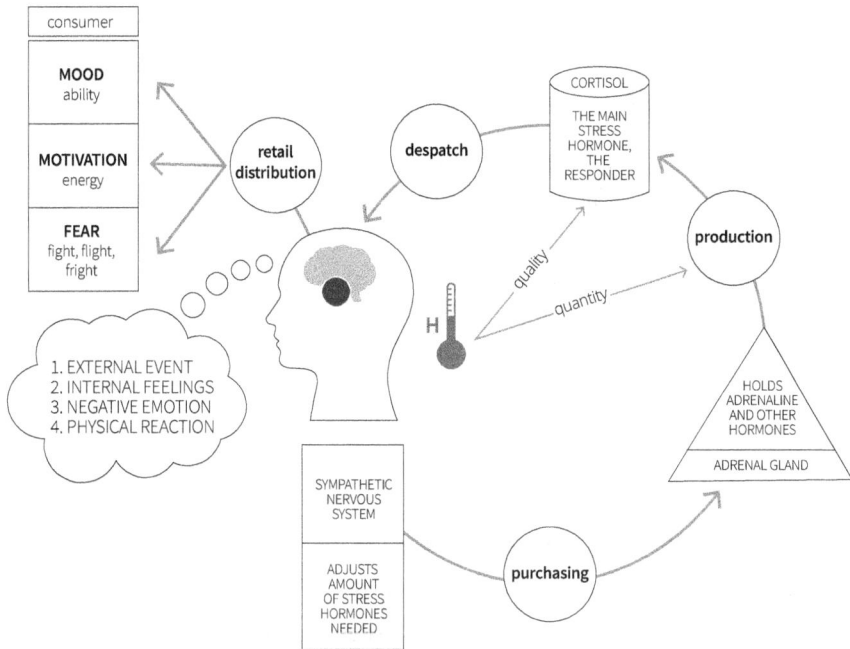

Figure 6. Stress response

*Within a business context, the stress response workflow
through event, feeling, emotion and reaction*

As a starting point for healthy body–healthy mind, I had decided to make a serious commitment to exercise and diet, something I was historically very on and off with. I started running for the first time ever, at age 50. The clarity and the energy that the endorphin kick provides is incredible. I have heard it called nature's home-brewed opiate – the runner's high – and I can see and feel why.

I was now on the way with physical improvement.

Traditional medicine referred me down a path of seeing a psychiatrist to assess for potential anxiety. It was a valuable experience – I met a great guy who I saw a number of times and who became a sort of personal coach, someone who really helped me see and think differently from what had been for some time a very solo perspective. But alas, there was no answer, no anxiety or depression diagnosis, however there was some great holistic advice.

I was also referred to a psychologist, and also an approach that uses eye movement (or something) to stimulate the emotional centres of the brain to address specific trauma responses (or something). Apparently you need to have a trauma for it to work. No result, so nothing there either.

By this time, my interest directed me to reading book after book, from one of my favourites in Sarah Wilson's *First, We Make The Beast Beautiful* to others that were 'next level' let's say, yet they helped me think differently, such as Ben Angel's *Unstoppable* and Dave Asprey's *Game Changers*, among others.

Reading and experience has allowed me to learn many things, however a condition many of these authors describe as 'brain fog' became a lightbulb moment for me – something I now define for myself as procrastination and intermittent immobility.

An online article in UK-based *Medical News Today* says that, 'brain fog can make a person feel as if the processes of thinking, understanding, and remembering are not working as they should'.[6] Boom! Now I was getting somewhere. This is how I was feeling at that time in my life. I was onto something, and I decided non-traditional medicine was worth a try. I sought advice from functional medicine and naturopathy practitioners.

What I like about naturopathy and functional medicine is you can test to ascertain a cause, rather than heading straight to treating a symptom first, as traditional medicine may seek to do. Obviously, I'm referring to non-critical interventions here, and no offence to

---

6   Sissons, C. *Medical News Today.* Online. June 2019.

my doctor friends – I respect what you do and will always value what you do.

I undertook a few tests, including the Cortisol Awakening Response (CAR) test which found I would wake up off the charts in terms of my 'awakening profile', but within 30 minutes I would start to decline or crash as opposed to continuing to rise (to a point) to deal with the day and what it throws at you. In layman's terms, my adrenal function was depleted after being in the front-line defending at scale and for such a long time.

I had nothing much left in the tank. It also explained why I hadn't slept properly for a very long time.

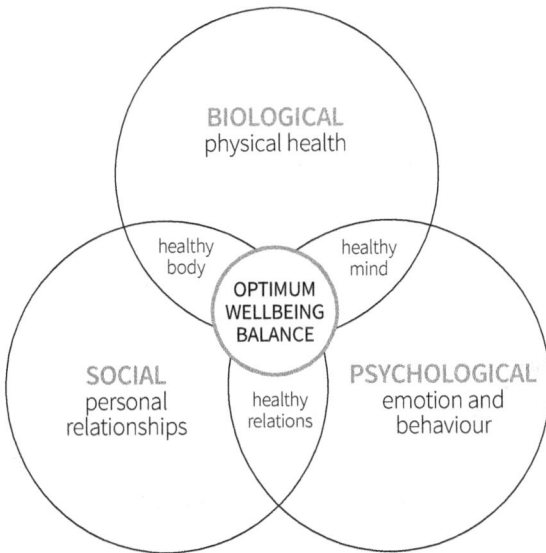

Figure 7. Healthy body, healthy mind

An adaptation of The Psychosocial Biological Model illustrating the optimum wellbeing balance, a metric that can be interpreted for both individual and organisational health

I consumed a six-month course of adrenal rebuilders to regenerate my adrenal function, to combat fatigue and exhaustion, and to optimise my cortisol-producing ability. I consumed shorter courses of other supplements to maintain healthy blood sugar levels, to enable metabolism, and to activate the calming neurotransmitters.

Without hesitation I embraced practitioner-approved supplements as a mitigation strategy. Within a week I felt positively different, and by the second week any doubts I may still have had about naturopathy had gone. By the third week I felt freaking amazing!

And through maintaining a balance of naturopathy, practitioner-approved supplements, nootropics and regular exercise and diet discipline, I still do. I feel unleashed. A line has been drawn in the sand again. I have my mojo back.

* * *

Like developing any strategy, if you don't know what success looks like – or you know but you can't seem to find a way to get going – go deep into the data; all the answers are usually in front of you. Make sure you not only ask the right questions, ask a lot of them so you can move from problem to solution rather than being stuck in the middle somewhere, accepting mediocrity.

And just in case you think that a compelling health strategy only belongs at home, it doesn't. A personal wellbeing strategy is the ultimate enabler of your contribution in the workplace or boardroom.

YOUR MINDSHIFT:
Knowing what really counts

How you 'show up' is really a representation of your physical and mental wellbeing. Here are 10 strategies that will minimise the impact of stressors dominating you. Manage the *cause* rather than having to deal with lingering *effect*.

1. **Failure precedes success.**
    This is about how you 'deal' with failure. Learning from it is deriving from the process rather than the result, and finding the motivator to do things differently that can really change results.

2. **Challenge is business as usual.**
    Embrace this new world. It is what it is, and there are millions of other people dealing with it also.

3. **Emotional strength.**
    Slowing down allows you time to deliberately reason with data to influence your decision-making.

4. **Work/life balance.**
    Working 12 hours a day doing meaningful and rewarding work is more sustainable than battling through six hours a day at something that's killing your soul. There's no rule; you must work out your own balance.

5. **Breaking point.**
    Recognise and remove the triggers that tip you over the edge. Usually it's various degrees (or not) of commitment, capacity and capability – yours and theirs.

6. **Have a compelling reason.**
   Focus your time and energy on doing something you enjoy and are passionate about, or at least create a plan that will achieve this within a finite period. This also goes for people you hang out with!

7. **Sleep it off.**
   Adequate sleep is the best way to refresh the brain, maintain physical wellbeing and respond to stress. Sleep is brain fuel. If you think you might need medical intervention, seek out the help you need.

8. **Get the blood pumping.**
   Not only is exercise important for physical wellbeing from a stress perspective, it stimulates chemicals in the brain that improve your mood and motivation, also stimulating memory and learning.

9. **Be mindful.**
   Take consistent device-free time outs to remove yourself from your environment – stressful or otherwise – and just breathe yourself to a clearer head.

10. **Someone to bounce off.**
    It doesn't necessarily need to be a mentor, just somebody you trust who you can download to and seek a different view from to inform yours. Maybe it's just a positive person to hang out with.

FOUR

PUTTING PEOPLE BEFORE PROFITS

UNDERSTANDING TRUST AND ITS IMPORTANCE

Trust is an organisation's lifeline. It is one of the most fundamental resources a business leader has. It is both an internal and external imperative.

In a social context, trust refers to a situation whereby one party (the trustor) is willing to rely on the actions of another party (the trustee).

In a traditional organisational context, the employer (trustor) will voluntarily abandon control over the actions performed by the employee (trustee) on the basis of the employee successfully executing their responsibilities.

Stay with me.

Here is how it *really* plays out. The employee (now the trustor) will voluntarily abandon any reservations around deploying discretionary effort and will go above and beyond for the employer (trustee) if the employer has committed to recognising and rewarding effort with remuneration, skills development and career advancement. Sometimes it is simply authentic recognition that will enable discretionary effort.

Disengagement arises when the trustee does not behave as desired.

Like we flipped the above definition of trust, it is also necessary to flip the traditional myopic leadership narrative around your business, your vision or your strategy for example, and instead empower your people to deliver on all of those business-critical things for you.

In this chapter I propose that people are your ultimate enablers. We dig deeper into the concept of aligned, capable and engaged people being an output of successful leadership rather than simply a collection of skills that are nice to have.

OPTIMISING YOUR CHANCES OF PRODUCING PROFITS WITH ACE PEOPLE

Aligned, *capable* and *engaged* people (ACE people) will be your ultimate enablers, and more so in crisis management.

Successful leaders can receive additional effort through first prioritising a specific picture around what success looks like for their people, knowing that this underpins momentum and enables business success to follow.

In any context, there is no capacity for disengaged and/or underperforming colleagues, so don't be afraid of making the tough decisions.

During a previous engagement leading an aggressive exit and wind-down in order to stop multi-million-dollar losses inside an international construction business, I didn't quite get the people situation right. It took me a second attempt to do so.

From day one this is how my internal and external people management plan rolled out:

1. Communicated with all staff as a group and told them how it was. ✓
2. Respectfully exited redundant staff and reduced fixed overhead costs. ✓
3. Collaborated with unions on an industrial relations strategy. ✓
4. Removed the business from unprofitable, high-risk projects. ✓
5. Renegotiated supply chain relationships to meet all liabilities. ✓
6. Collated all legal and litigation risks and resolved them one at a time. ✓
7. Replaced project staff on two distressed projects. ✗

Here is where I made the mistake. I trusted the long-term people now managing the distressed projects, the people who purported to have the most project knowledge and valuable subcontractor relationships. Wrong.

I took the path of least resistance. With hindsight I learned they were part of the wider cultural problem and that they disengaged the stakeholders who were critical to partnering with me in a turnaround. But dealing with numerous stakeholders and complex financial issues is not an excuse.

I thought I had made all the tough decisions at the start. It only took a few weeks to experience an escalation of risk and loss on these projects that indicated I obviously hadn't. Fortunately, I had the opportunity to activate a different, albeit belated, strategy. There is no doubt that the final outcome for these two projects and the business was delayed by more than two months.

* * *

As leaders, we cannot afford to take the path of least resistance. We need to pre-qualify the people we are partnering with. When you are in crisis, you need your A-team. Simple. We need to be assured that accountability, authority and delegation will enable optimum performance and risk management.

And for your people, it's not all about bonuses and increased salary. Sure, this helps, and there are passengers out there – it's delusional to think there are not. However, a crisis – or some issue way out of left field – is often the development opportunity that will provide your most capable, engaged and aligned people with what they need to develop and get to their own *next*.

In the context of crisis, it is critical each one of your people knows exactly what is in it for them every single day. It's about helping them understand where the crisis sits, how the business is performing, and how that impacts them – keeping the lines of communication open, involving them in your turnaround strategy, and articulating their role in it.

Amid business crisis your people still want to know what their *next* looks like – are they being challenged and provided with personal and career-enhancing development opportunities as a result of the crisis management? Despite the fine line the business is travelling, promote it as a learning and development experience. You will be surprised at the number of people who will be excited by this opportunity for unique fast-tracked development.

Personalise the business strategy and don't isolate your people from it. And provide advance warning before fundamental divergence so there are no surprises.

And don't forget recognition and, if the post-crisis environment affords it, reward. Don't think that discretionary effort should go unrecognised or unrewarded just because you have been in unusual circumstances.

When you are deep in crisis, here are **five fundamental people questions** to ask yourself:

1. **ACE people.** Do I have people who *can*, *know* and *want*? Who are *aligned*, *capable* and *engaged*?

2. **Holding on.** Do I have the same old people doing more of the same, just holding on in hope of a better outcome?

3. **Contractors.** Do I have access to specialist contractors or freelancers to help me economically build my bridge to *next*?

4. **Experts.** Do I have external advisors who I can rely on to get down and dirty when we need to?

5. **Meaning and purpose.** Have I told everyone what is in it for each one of them?

WHAT DO YOUR PEOPLE REALLY WANT?

How many times have you asked yourself *what's in it for me?*

From a business perspective, how often do you think your peers or your direct reports ask this very same question? Personal context is everything, and most people use this as the filter through which to evaluate their work environment. In every corner of our daily being this subconscious risk–reward enquiry informs effort and underpins output in almost everything we do. It is a very simple concept, yet one that is often overlooked.

From a business perspective, being able to clearly articulate what is in it for your people is fundamental to successful strategy execution. It is also an imperative that will define your personal success, development and advancement; and ultimately your recognition – or not – as an engaging and authentic leader.

To assume your people will simply fall in behind business processes and provide optimum performance is unrealistic. Whether it be a factory worker, an admin assistant or an executive team, before they willingly provide additional effort they will want to know what their professional development looks like over what period of time, and how their responsibilities will optimise their experience and maximise their future opportunities and remuneration.

If it is not clear to them, it's likely their effort will be simply compliant rather than discretionary, that their approach will be disengaged rather than engaged, and that their commitment will be short rather than long term. Instead of building a strong and sustainable business around a workforce of enabled people, you will simply be fulfilling an uncompelling 'bums on seats' strategy that you hope will deliver a bottom-line return, indicative of the Holding On to Fail Strategy that we refer to in chapter 2.

Once your people know what's in it for them and they know they have the capability and the back-up to execute well, and they are engaged in the purpose and are aligned to the process, you have every opportunity to optimise and maximise whatever it is you are looking to achieve.

The following graphic illustrates the distinction between and the benefit of collectively aligned, capable and engaged people and the impact the right people will have on strategy execution and business optimisation. Don't be afraid to privately allocate your perception of people capability to the categories in figures 8 and 9. For me, a visual representation helped me understand what lay in front of me, and what inroads I was making progressively.

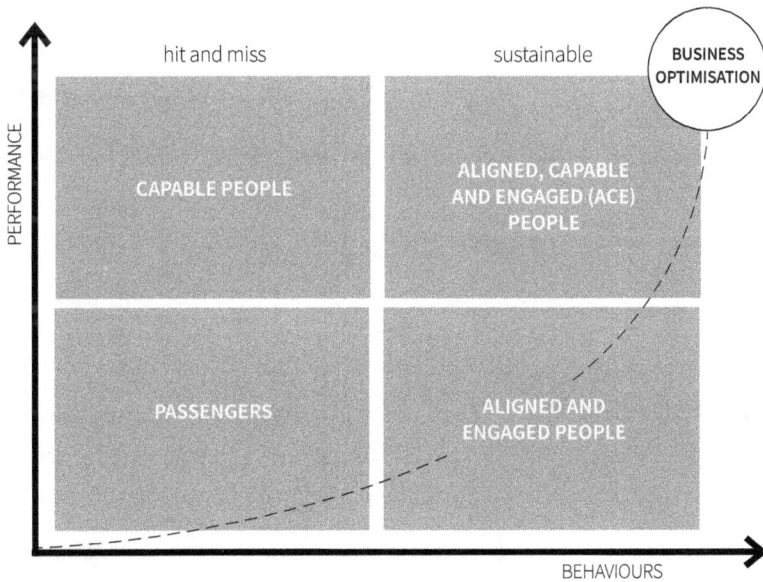

Figure 8. ACE people
Sustainable business outcomes enabled by aligned, capable and engaged people, as opposed to hit-and-miss outcomes delivered by capable people usually in isolation of the organisation's bigger picture

Successful leaders know their people are their ultimate enablers. They will prioritise building a specific picture as to what success looks like for their people, knowing this is an imperative in delivering the business's goals.

From an employee perspective this is their fundamental question. Gone is the one-dimensional view around job security; it's about each one of them getting to their own *next*.

Do you know what your people really want out of their role? What each one of their goals looks like, over what period, and with what resources you can and perhaps cannot provide? Can you attribute a 'value' to the role your people play in your organisation's bigger picture, or rather, how your people's desired success will align with the business's strategy? While some 'big brands' are sought out as CV enhancement, mostly it is the people they will work with and the development available that informs what's in it for them.

Give people their *next* and they might just give you their best.

PUTTING YOUR PEOPLE FIRST

The concept of people before profit originated from an Irish left-wing socialist political party, and more recently the American 2018 Business Roundtable declaring that a company's purpose is to benefit 'all stakeholders (customers, employees, communities and the environment)'[1], seeming to depart from a long-held corporate belief that businesses ultimately exist only to serve shareholders.

The relevant perspective on putting people before profits is centred on generating profit *as a result of* putting people first. It is an acknowledgement that engaged people produce profits before processes, products or brands will, for example. Returning to the

---

1   Stanford Graduate School of Business. *People Before Profits: A New American Credo?* Online. September 2019.

'what's in it for me' question, allowing your people and their capabilities to inform the planning and execution of your business's strategy is putting people before profit. It will produce discretionary effort and it will deliver commercial upside.

This is all about building a critical mass of capable people to enable business sustainability, rather than a few superstars carrying the weight of business success or, alternatively, attempting to micromanage 'bums on seats' to a common goal which, really, is like herding cats. Often the largest resource you will have in business is people, so use their collective productivity rather than a perceived individual capability to achieve your goals.

It took me a while to get to this thinking – perhaps I needed to experience a few more of the downs rather than ups in business. It wasn't until faced with extreme adversity that I experienced the 'people before profits' lightbulb moment.

* * *

In the post-GFC turmoil, as CEO of APM we were ducking and weaving commercial and contracting risk left, right and centre. We thought we were successful because we'd maintained a marketable reputation, had great people, enjoyed a full pipeline of projects and were still producing profit, all while the world was falling apart around us.

Then, out of left field through a series of subcontractor insolvencies that nearly nailed us to the wall, we were bleeding cash through losses and overheads at a rate of $1M a month. It wasn't until month six of this that we really started to achieve turnaround traction. It was a massive ship to turn at that stage.

The most important initiative which contributed to our turnaround success was that each of our people knew exactly what was in it for them every single day. And, from an external perspective, each one of our clients knew what project success looked like for us and for them every single month. We prioritised internal and external people firstly and equally.

It was never about telling someone they were lucky to have a job in an uncertain environment. It was always about helping them understand:

- where the business was at and how that would impact them from a livelihood perspective
- what role they could play in the business turnaround
- how their success in this role would not only keep the business and their livelihood afloat, it would provide valuable skills that would add value to them.

We personalised our strategy, and we didn't isolate them from it. There was always advance warning before fundamental divergence so there were no surprises. And despite the fine line the business was travelling, we promoted this as a learning experience for our people.

To survive with a diminishing pipeline, we did have to lose some staff; however, again, this wasn't a surprise. By constantly communicating what was in it for the people involved, we only transacted one redundancy alongside 53 other voluntary resignations and/or outplacements.

* * *

The success of any initiative comes from backing up good communication with decisive action; it then becomes a cycle that introduces learnings and outcomes, with constant and consistent 'what's in it for them' communication.

Reward and recognition helps, but when livelihoods are at stake we all want to know what's coming our way, and if we don't, we will leave and land somewhere that we don't have to worry about this.

Whatever the business environment, your people want to know what their *next* looks like: are they being challenged and provided every opportunity to advance, to climb their own ladder, to be exposed to the right leaders? If they are, you can be assured you are optimising and maximising your people.

There is no way we would have transformed our losses without an authentic people-engagement strategy.

RIGHT PEOPLE

Successful leaders prioritise building a specific picture around what success looks like for their people, knowing this underpins momentum and business success. They know that understanding their employees' personal context is fundamental to attracting discretionary effort.

They also have this level of engagement in place from day one so that should a crisis eventuate, special projects arise or performance needs to lift a gear, there is no mistaking who will seek to escalate their own efforts in support of the business.

In any context there is no capacity for disengaged or under-performing colleagues. In a perfect world, we don't have them; however, we all know they exist. It is the opponents, the resistors and the separatists who sit inside our organisations that will undermine discretionary effort.

The following graphic is adapted from Marc Stigter and Sir Cary Cooper's *Solving The Strategy Delusion*, to stimulate your thinking around where your organisational 'engagement' may sit.

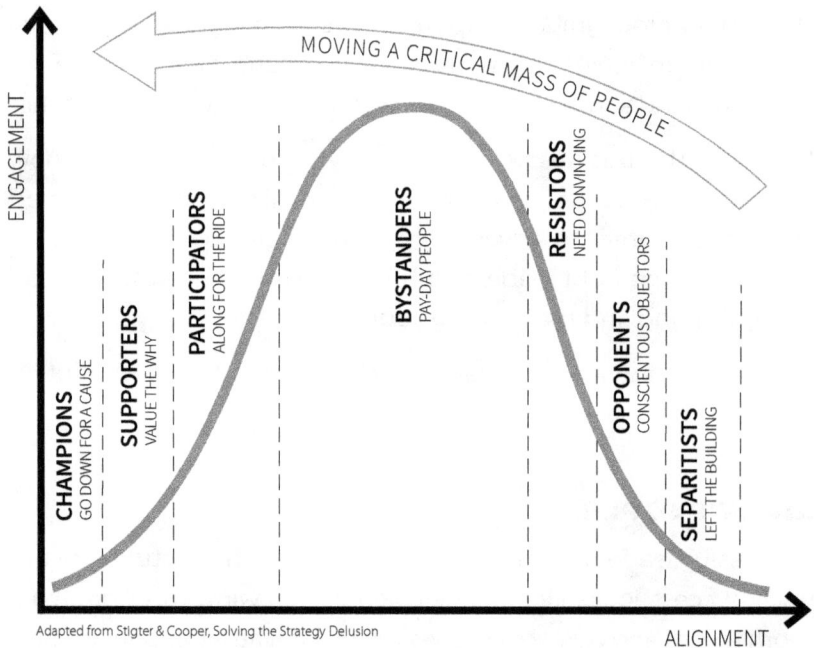

Figure 9. Motivating your ACE people

You will always have a champion or two, however often it is the supporters and participators who will leave because the bystanders and beyond are allowed to remain or are not developed by you

A few years ago I was engaged to undertake a high-level review of business reporting and financial forecasts so as to bring relative certainty, or not, to the sustainability of a New Zealand business's Australian branch. The board had been receiving colourful reports and positive dialogue around revenue upside and risk-mitigation strategies, yet reality was showing decreased opportunities and declining profitability.

I was about to experience the most extraordinary example of a toxic, excluding and isolated culture. In hindsight, perhaps it wasn't even a culture, simply a collection of people sitting in an office. But to be fair to many, this was an ingrained attitude promoted by only a few within the local leadership ranks. The rot had well and truly set in.

This business was allowed to exist autonomously, despite three consecutive years of underperformance. There really wasn't any meaningful ParentCo intervention until a new CEO was appointed, however it was too late as the local management team had been allowed to exist like the proverbial rudderless ship.

The business development manager couldn't secure adequate revenue in the most opportunistic three-year period in that decade, the previous estimating manager made fundamental and high-cost errors, the construction manager by admission 'didn't do numbers', and the general manager usually had his office door shut.

In the 12 months prior to my stepping in, 18 out of 30 staff were replaced, every project was delayed and losing money, project reports were inaccurate, incomplete or contingent upon a future event, and there were more legal issues than days in the week. In each of my confidential discussions, every finger pointed to the (local) top, and all but two of the 27 staff that I met were disengaged to the point of actively seeking exit. Apparently, this was going on for three years.

I won't go on, as it's not fair to the majority of staff who were not responsible for creating or leading this culture, however my point is the wrong people with inadequate skills were in jobs that were beyond them, a predicament which took the business to the brink of insolvency among $6M in project losses. This amount was compensated by the offshore ParentCo as it wound down and retreated from Australia (indicative of a very different and honourable culture led by two of the local Directors, I might add), an event

I am reasonably certain was one of the factors fundamental in the ultimate financial failure of the ParentCo some 12 months later.

It all started with people.

* * *

To attract the right people with the right skills, and place them in the right jobs at the right time, you must look beyond just the quantitative perspective of staffing. You must consider more qualitatively the emerging skills that will be required by the industry, and your offering.

You can have the best graphic representation of a skills matrix or a great talent acquisition strategy, however without effective workforce planning – and by effective, I mean relevant and dynamic – you may simply be creating an unproductive process fulfilling a current need to increase headcount. A 'bums on seats' strategy.

We all have varying degrees of people management experience – at whatever level – and we willingly take a risk or trust our ability in hiring talent or outsourcing skills. There is nothing wrong with this; it is what we do. It is highly likely you will know more about your industry and you will be prepared to take a risk in forecasting change – where you see technology taking your industry, your business and your people, for example. Maybe it's the influence of competition, regulation or geopolitical factors?

My point is that we consider managed risks every day in business, so why is it that often when hiring we look for comfort in traditional roles and, perhaps, yesterday's capability? In attempting to hedge your bets against failure, you could be missing out on capability that could create substantial value.

The following image provides a generic framework for thinking through the skills transformation from *now* to *next*. We transition from the point of 'old business' – which might be confronting for some – and we seek to create a progressive mindset around the necessity to stay in front of the game, as your current business will at some stage be a thing of the past, probably more quickly than you think.

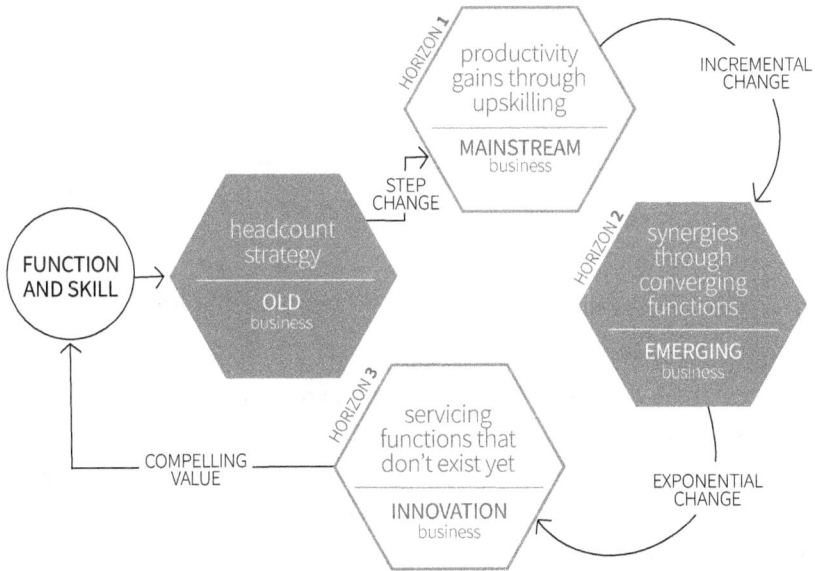

Figure 10. Function–skill horizon

Understanding the business's horizon and taking responsibility for developing people capability and organisation value

Most leaders know what kind of talent they are looking for in the moment, but few think ahead to how their people's skills will align with their long-term strategy.

ORGANISATIONAL F.E.E.L.I.N.G

This is not a book about people and culture per se, however we know by now that everything starts and stops with people. Everything we engage in – the strategy sensing, the risk mitigation, the operational intervention, the stakeholder management, the reporting and governance, whatever it is – is all about people creating this success (or not) within a culture or environment that enables it (or not).

The environment within which this is enabled is the *culture*, derived from the Latin *colere*, which means to tend to the earth and grow, or cultivate and nurture. There are many modern interpretations, however for me in relation to business it is simply 'how a team behaves when no-one is looking'.

If culture is *the how*, your backstory, your specific internal narrative becomes *your why*. This connection is culture's reinforcing loop.

While a culture is unique to every organisation, the foundation of what enables a culture to thrive is the extent to which employees are empowered to be engaged, feel valued, and be heard. This is where leadership comes in, ensuring there is an alignment between the organisation's bigger picture, its reason for being and the values and behaviours its people desire to live and work by.[2]

This equilibrium – while hard work – is absolutely achievable, however it's very tough to maintain this balance through crisis management as it is through periods of turmoil that the culture is put to the test. When fundamental decisions are being made and personal livelihoods are at stake, this is when you will really know how good, or not, your culture is and what your likelihood of success might be.

---

2   Baumgartner, N. 'Build A Culture That Aligns With People Values'. *Harvard Business Review*. 2020.

Ultimately, we are talking about employee engagement (or disengagement), and the connection that joins people and culture brings us back full circle to whether or not your people know what's in it for them. The connector in this exchange is leadership and their ability to maintain organisational and individual health when trying to stop the bleeding – to advocate a feeling of control that identifies stress is an inevitable part of the current circumstance while maintaining an unwavering commitment to the end game. Easier said than done!

This **organisational F.E.E.L.I.N.G** according to, and for the benefit of, your people should include the following **seven top-down mind shifts to building a modern culture**:

1. **Feedback** opens the door for growth and learning, and is necessary to optimise individual and organisational performance. Setting reasonable goals and standards for achievement will help keep everyone appropriately challenged and focused only if the leaders are also open to feedback and change as a result. This is a real *walk the talk* scenario – you need to meaningfully lead this open two-way dialogue on a fairly regular basis.

2. **Empowerment** in relation to culture is both sides of trust, that which is both given and received. Trust is a high-value form of organisational capital, the environment whereby your people can fully realise their own capacity and power as given by you, and their commitment and capability as received by you in return. This win–win partnership model is what will underpin discretionary effort.

3. **Experimentation** is not about a lack of discipline or 'loosely' adding layers of risk to your current situation. It is about giving permission to ask *what if* rather than *what is?* In an organisation where your backs are already to the wall,

encouraging thinking outside of the safe 'this is how we always do it' square to 'we are where we are because we always do it this way – let's do it differently' circle is not usually obstructed by tools and technology but more so traditional behaviours, beliefs and values.

4. **Learning** is about redefining failures, and removing the anxiety created by surprises. It is about allowing a collaborative *what next* rather than *what the ... ?* Often, a crisis will unravel at speed, and your ability to predict when and how often risk will occur is uncertain at best. A culture of throwing the baby out with the bath water, of anger and detachment when something comes out of left field, will not allow anyone to learn from it. Consider FAIL as your First Attempt In Learning.

5. **Information** gathering or having a data-driven mindset enables fact-based decision-making, justifying risk management objectives and actions. The challenge however is promoting data as a path to performance management without your people feeling that big brother is watching. Celebrating quick wins, showcasing *that was then, this is now*, and using the data to build a picture of what success looks like will create a proactive and engaged workforce that has a greater understanding of how they are performing and insight into where improvements can be made.

6. **Nurturing** your people to maximise their potential is the quickest road to your success as a leader and in maximising output as an organisation. Talent, hard work and luck are important in helping people reach their peak but are insufficient in enabling them to continue to perform on a consistent basis without professional and personal development. You need the balance of nature *and* nurture.

7. **Gratitude** is appreciation for effort. When people feel appreciated and grateful, they're willing to commit more effort to the cause, to their colleagues, to finding solutions, to being loyal sometimes even at a cost to themselves. This generous respect will assist in building a path to perseverance and to motivating your people to see it through deep in the trenches alongside you.

Choosing my words carefully, I don't recommend we leave behind the traditional culture of honesty, integrity and encouragement, for example. I do suggest however that once we have constructed this foundation of trust, let's take it to the next level and accelerate a more self-sufficient culture of creativity, experimentation and empowerment, to name a few.

Or let me ask you this: how will you keep up with the pace of technology and disruption, the demands of an agile business model, and the ever more socially-conscious values of the millennial workforce which desires to leave a positive impact on the world?

MASTER MINDS

You will notice I often use the phrase 'seeing, thinking, planning and acting differently'. As a mature-age business school student a few years ago, learning about this was a lightbulb moment for me that remains etched in my mind as vividly as it was scribbled on the whiteboard that day. It was as if I now had permission to step sideways and start looking from the *outside-in* at what was a very narrow industry and a self-imposed, aggressively competitive, one-dimensional paradigm.

It actually isn't as deep as it sounds. It is more so a realisation or learning for me personally that there is a different perspective out there. While I admit it took some time to entrench this different way, and I do not proclaim to have 'nailed it', it certainly was a foundation for a mind shift for me.

I believe it is this very concept of seeing, thinking, planning and acting differently that underpins the mindset of the classic entrepreneur. However, it also explains a process that enables you to optimise and maximise what (any) success could really look like. And it opens the door to collaboration, to co-creation, to partnerships, and on a more individual and personal level, to mentoring.

Most people build their network passively over time through proximity, with a few outliers in their mix. Unless you have been deliberate about your networking, the vast majority of people you know probably belong to the same community, field or industry as you. This situation may seem innocent enough, however that inadvertent short-sightedness can put you at risk of not being able to see, think, plan and act differently.

You need to have a balance of both 'bonding capital' and 'bridging capital' – relationships based respectively on your commonalities (bonding) and relationships built across differences (bridging).[3] You must take the definition of balance in this case to reflect the necessity of having more than one perspective.

* * *

Back in the APM post-GFC turmoil when we were bleeding cash at the rate of $1M a month, I was fortunate to have three great mentors.

One was Global Strategy Advisor Marc Stigter PhD, my recent Melbourne Business School Program Director who had turned on the see, think, plan and act differently light. The other was David

---

3   Putnam, R.D. *Bowling Alone: The collapse and revival of American community.* 2000.

Marriner, a highly experienced and successful businessman, investor and property developer who at that time also happened to be a client. And my third partner in crime was Kari Rummukainen, my joint-venture partner.

Marc was a formal mentor supporting organisational strategy. David provided the client stakeholder perspective, and Kari the contractor cashflow perspective – these latter two were the subtle 'sounding board' mentors who also had skin in the game.

Business turnaround was the strategy, there was no question. It was a matter of survival.

Marc provided me the structure to collect my at times anxious thinking. We created a war room and set about defending. We went through many success and fail scenarios at both personal and organisational levels, producing a $7M turnaround in nine months.

While David was invested from the perspective of being a client, he had the option of enforcing the contract, and exiting, which would inflict great pain on myself and the business. Instead we set about fortnightly meetings over breakfast, discussing the progress of the business's turnaround strategy. He shared his business experiences of the previous 30-plus years and not only validated our turnaround strategy but also provided considerable moral and financial support when the aggression of the GFC was unloading at a great rate. An authentic friendship developed that not only ultimately underpinned our turnaround financially through a handshake loan, it is a personal one that continues with strength to this day.

In the cut and thrust of business turnaround, the aggressive subcontractor facing cashflow management back-up advice that Kari provided was great motivation to keep pushing back. Sometimes you need someone to second guess the daily fundamental sustainability questions, to push you, to extract and motivate your determination. To convince you that it is okay to say no.

One provided me strategic structure, the other two provided me affirmation and motivation.

When I had successfully completed the third and final consolidation phase almost three years down the track, I had gained deep insights as to what success looked like for both myself and the business. Without the benefits of numerous external perspectives, without seeing and thinking differently, I would not have enhanced the business through turnaround; or myself, through transacting an exit and then building a successful corporate advisory proposition.

* * *

If you are someone who seeks to benefit from mentoring, I suggest you:

1. put together a group of people you can turn to for advice when you need it, and consider who might really push your thought boundaries

2. create both informal and formal short-term and long-term relationships – mix it up (and don't put any pressure on the informal)

3. nurture relationships with the people whose perspectives you respect; if it's not working for you, don't be a time waster and politely withdraw

4. consider how you may be able to 'give back' in some way, being mindful that all get and no give might impact the levels of authentic engagement

5. value the advice and take action.

Mentoring is not reserved for business professionals. It adds value at so many levels, and more to the point successful mentoring is focused initially on the person, rather than their career or relevant 'whatever' situation, in order to first get to what makes someone tick.

Being a mentor is a position of privilege. Should you decide to accept that privilege someday, here are **10 ways to successfully engage in mentoring**:

1. **Work backwards.** Start with the end in mind. What do they want out of this? And why?

2. **Take the bigger picture view.** Focus on the whole person, not just their career.

3. **Unleash the enabler.** Co-create their compelling story around a purpose. What makes them tick?

4. **Don't force it.** Don't try to build a new model – draw out their ideal self.

5. **Be genuine.** Provide empathetic acknowledgement – don't be an expert or a hero.

6. **Cut out the fluff**. It's okay to politely say 'so what?' Don't forget that you have a responsibility to add value, not just to listen.

7. **Allow discovery.** Reflect often, facilitating deeper insights. It's okay to change direction.

8. **Check back in.** Are you moving their needle or just listening and telling stories? Check often.

9. **Curate learning.** It's not about you, it's about them learning not only from your experience but their own deep insights.

10. **Create a feedback loop.** Set some tasks to measure your success in co-creating enduring value.

YOUR MINDSHIFT:
See yourself as an enabler

1. **People first.**
   To assume your people will simply fall in behind business processes and provide optimum performance is delusional thinking.

2. **Make it compelling.**
   Your people want to know what is in it for them. Personal context is the filter through which they will evaluate their work environment and commitment to it. Don't leave them guessing.

3. **Career development.**
   A culture of personal development and opportunity creates momentum and builds critical mass around a group of enablers, rather than a few superstars who may carry the weight of business success.

4. **Skill fit.**
   A people-centric environment will co-create what success looks like for the individual, appreciating their skill fit, acknowledging their skill gap, and committing to what, who and how they will be supported.

5. **Mix it up.**
   Be prepared to make a decision that will change a specific environment. Make an impact that improves individual wellbeing as the momentum it will generate is invaluable.

6. **ACE people.**

   Should a crisis eventuate, it will only be your aligned, capable and engaged people who will seek to truly ramp up their own efforts in support of themselves and the business.

7. **People innovation.**

   You must look beyond just the quantitative perspective of 'bums on seats' staffing and consider more qualitatively the emerging skills that will be required by the industry and your business in the future.

8. **Let go.**

   There is a reason you are where you are – holding on to now irrelevant strategy and people hoping that things will 'just change' is unrealistic. While it starts at the top, your people are your ultimate enablers.

9. **Keep it real.**

   Personalise your strategies. Don't isolate your people from them, and provide advance warning before fundamental divergence so that there are no surprises, and ultimately, disengagement.

10. **Skills horizon.**

    Most leaders know what kind of talent they are looking for in the moment, but few think ahead to how their people's skills will align with their long-term strategy.

FIVE

DEVELOPING GREAT PEOPLE

ASSUMING THAT PEOPLE WILL SIMPLY FALL IN BEHIND BUSINESS PROCESSES AND PRODUCE GREAT OUTCOMES IS DELUSIONAL THINKING

There was a traditional, and (hopefully) now outdated, mindset that a process is an organisation's ultimate lever. We know also that great people are developed by good leaders. It doesn't 'just happen'. While process is a critical success factor in enhancing business performance, optimum output is created by people in a culture that prioritises these people.

The intentional distinction used here between 'good' and 'great' is the obligation on today's leaders, regardless of business size or their management reach, to not only develop the next level of succession but to enhance it. Quite simply, to make it better.

As culture is – or should be – a top-down influence, it is leadership behaviour that determines not only team dynamics but also the recognition of the importance of people, based on displaying respect, encouraging learning, providing development, permitting empowerment, providing clarity, sharing values and promoting trust.

People are the central element of organisational change – strategies that focus on systems and structures alone will fail.

In order to improve people – and in turn business – performance, leaders and managers at all levels need to be actively hands-in alongside their people, implementing sustainable change. It's crucial for companies to constantly assess and improve their people leadership skills so they can strengthen employee development, promote career opportunity, maximise business productivity and ultimately grow their business.

In this chapter I will demonstrate that authentic and permissive leadership, a culture of engagement and development, as well as personal context from an employee perspective determines the extent of discretionary effort, which ultimately enables business success.

SHIFTING MINDSETS

Often to create change and get closer to a more desirable outcome, we need to give up on some of the behaviour and thinking (the attitudes) that have locked us into that previous suboptimal state.

The view you adopt for yourself profoundly affects the way you lead your life.[1] Across the spectrum of positive vs negative, of optimistic vs pessimistic, or of glass half full vs glass half empty, if we are to succeed in implementing enduring strategic change we need to first unlock the biases and unwillingness to innovate that are entrenched in a fixed mindset.

People with a growth mindset believe their ability to learn and accumulate intelligence will develop with time and experience. Successful people invest considerable time to develop a growth mindset, acquire new knowledge, learn new skills and change their perception in order to benefit their lives. They know that making small, continual improvements will compound over time and produce optimum results.

In a business context, a growth mindset is a collective belief that an organisation has the ability to do things differently, which is a critical foundation to the concept of co-creating different seeing, thinking, planning and acting.

To achieve enduring change, how do you change a mindset?

---

1   Dweck, C.S. *Mindset: Changing the way you think to fulfil your potential.* 2012.

It may not be as hard as it sounds. As one's mindset originates from our own set of powerful beliefs, we can change these beliefs when they no longer serve us or enable us to achieve our goals, as the following adaptation from the Kubler-Ross Change Curve (or Stages of Grief) illustrates.

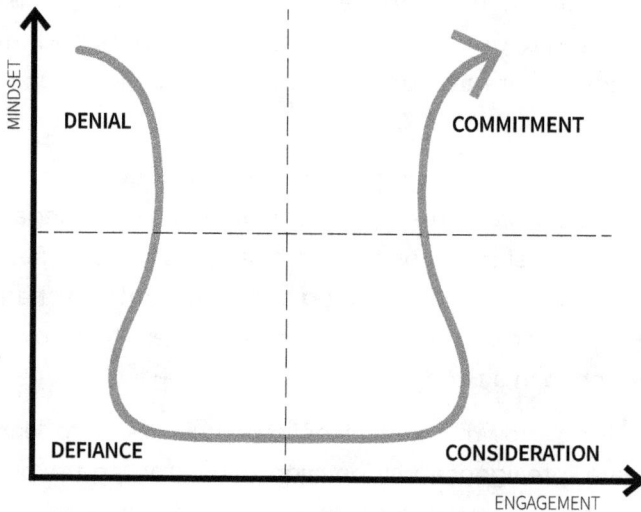

Figure 11. MindShift
*The emotional impact on your current mindset
brought about by a journey through different experiences.*

From the perspective of overcoming organisational inertia and in order to get to a collective growth mindset, consider these **five strategies for shifting fixed thinking:**

1. **Create a compelling story.** In creating a compelling strategy from your people's perspective first, their knowing what's in it for them becomes the critical first step in changing thinking, and to receiving additional effort.

2. **Encourage self-awareness.** Acknowledge the strength of diversity in experiences and skills, and applaud the strengths and weaknesses that will make a difference.

3. **Provide a learning environment.** Encourage self-discovery. Promote the benefits of learning and growing and provide access to mentored development or structured learning that will add individual value.

4. **Recognise and reward.** In addition to discretionary effort among the operational day to day, the psychological contract you have asked your people to execute is worth something. Put some metrics in place and respond to them. This will accumulate collective momentum for change.

5. **Share in successes.** Aside from the more materialistic reward and recognition, quite simply celebrate both individual and team achievement. Seeing others succeed 'releases' their mind to the possibilities available for them.

A DESK IS A DANGEROUS PLACE

'VUCA' is a concept that originated with students at the US Army War College to describe the volatility, uncertainty, complexity, and ambiguity of the world after the Cold War – a 40-something-year period of post–World War II open rivalry between the US and the Soviet Union. While VUCA describes four different challenges and four different responses, it quite simply describes geopolitical chaos and serves as a warning to think deep and hard before your next move.

Most of our leaders aren't consumed with organisational strategy but are instead overwhelmed with managing day-to-day operational challenges.[2]

---

2   Stigter, M. and Cooper, C. *Solving the Strategy Delusion.* 2015.

The truly good leaders know it is their responsibility to establish the foundation, or the vision, for what success needs to look like. The truly good leaders will also know that by co-creating a compelling story with and for their people first, the odds of creating a sustainable and compelling strategy for the business are heavily stacked in their favour.

If leaders cannot inspire action, where will it come from? (Apart from a compelling business story such as the one you are reading of course ... !)

Strategic vision doesn't simply come from a business case or a presentation, it comes from the people. In fact, meaningful strategy doesn't come from a whiteboard or an offsite Directors' weekend either. It evolves with and through your people.

Successful leaders create the building blocks from which thinking momentum originates, developing into purposeful strategy, meaningful metrics, optimum execution and successful outcomes.

Momentum must be generated at the company's centre of gravity, its core of people. The traditional leadership style legitimised by hierarchies, suit-and-tie 'power messages' and founded on top-down directives is increasingly being made redundant by inclusive, socially responsible leadership invested in collaboration over competition.

While those who wield power still shape the fate of a business, it's the astute ones who intend playing the 'long game' of leadership that know in today's VUCA environment a 'democratic dictatorship' is no longer adequate to maintain a competitive edge. They will actively strengthen connections to their teams and foster more creative space from which new ideas will evolve. To meet these demands, many of today's leaders may need to change their mindset and their behaviours.

Leaders will quite often talk about 'engaging their people'. Perhaps they're just focusing on the engaged people as it's the path of least resistance? Employees need to be fired up; they need to be given the chance to help shape the company's success. This is only going to happen if there is a leading figure who combines motivational skills with courage, while at the same time remaining humble and truly authentic.[3]

Here are a few other considerations to throw into the mix.

While a necessary focus, why not start seeing, thinking, planning and acting differently through focusing on the disengaged people first, the minority, the conscientious objectors, those that are way outside of left field? Why not bring them in to the 'land of co-creation' and see what they're thinking? Imagine the benefit that could bring once you engage with them, show them what's in it for them, realign their commitment and extract discretionary effort from them.

Then we are really building critical mass, we are not just playing a numbers game.

In the majority of cases leaders are selected to lead. Stating the obvious I know, however my point is that, importantly, leaders put themselves in this position; they execute a psychological contract – they want to be in 'this chair' and they want to be successful. They know they must engage, interact and intervene. They sign up knowing that they must embrace uncertainty and be excited by challenge and adversity.

It's about respecting and empowering people. It's about turning risk into opportunity. It's about being a progressive and authentic corporate citizen. It's about focusing ultimately on commercial

---

3   Najipoor-Schutte, K. *Harvard Business Manager*. Online. December 2018.

outcomes all of the time because there is always a bigger picture to be had and a better bottom line to be found.

Hanging onto yesterday's outcome is irrelevant today. Leaders must inspire action, and perhaps the most simple visual for us to consider is that sitting behind a desk is a very dangerous place from which to lead.

FOLLOWING GREAT LEADERS

There is a traditional view that an organisation's leaders create and direct strategy, Managers deliver it through operations, and subordinates followed the instructions of both. But in today's business environment of flatter, networked organisations collaborating across many verticals and geographies, we need to change traditional thinking and acknowledge that, in addition to leaders and managers, great followers exist, with an emerging-leader skillset of strategic and operational capability.

This is a deliberate departure from the leader-centric approach that dominates traditional thinking. Followers can be the arms and legs that promote and encourage discretionary effort. In a business setting, a follower or a champion is a non-traditional and positive description of an emerging leader. It is not a title and shouldn't be a label, more so a reminder that successful leadership at any level is based on support and succession.

Inextricably linked to the philosophy of people being our ultimate enablers, which we discussed in the previous chapter, is the concept that this critical mass of people is in fact a cohort of followers (notwithstanding that they sit at different levels on the ACE radar of alignment, capability and engagement). Successful leaders acknowledge the importance of understanding their followers better, and will acknowledge that followers can create better and distributed leadership at all levels of the organisation.

This is not a one-way, subservient street, however. Good followers invest time and energy in making informed decisions about who their leaders are and what they stand for. This is the big-picture view of leadership, one where leaders and followers co-create and co-exist for the betterment of the organisation, whether that be strategic sensing, strategy creation, operational deployment, people engagement or succession planning, to name just a few of the values this concept adds.

In terms of capability, the step from follower to leader does not need to be massive – and that's not to say that you need to or want to make that step. However, there are soft 'learned' skills which are a great place from which to become a great leader.

The **10 soft skills that define a successful leader** are:

1. **Resilience.** A skillset whereby organisational anxiety is effectively managed despite people sometimes being overworked, overwhelmed and challenged.

2. **Executive being.** How you are trusted and how you trust others; how you interact and communicate in an environment of pressure.

3. **Culture excitement.** Without being over the top, creating more involvement in workplace communities and building excitement and engagement.

4. **Relaxed agility.** Despite the complexity and ambiguity of change, an ability to respond quickly, effectively and competitively with relative calm.

5. **Multi-skilled.** Exposure to various job functions over time, collecting complementary skills and deeper organisational insights.

6. **Virtual collaborator.** Knowing when and how to manage co-created outcomes, whether in the same room or globally remote.

7. **Emotionally intelligent.** An authentic and empathetic 'emotions radar', optimising trusted relationships and meaningful engagement.

8. **Authentic connector.** Confidence and belief in your ability comes through authentic connection at all levels, both personally and professionally.

9. **Tough but fair.** The ability to respectfully and authentically engage in tough and critical conversations with a view to producing win–win outcomes.

10. **A co-creator.** Someone who participates in change as a collaborator rather than as a passenger alongside it.

GREAT PERFORMANCE STARTS WITH YOU

In order to avoid the lip service that people-facing initiatives often suffer and to succeed in delivering a compelling strategy for your people, you must think differently about the concept of performance management.

There is no doubt the current fast-paced, tech-driven business culture is building momentum around more dynamic, flexible and efficient ways of doing. However, the vast majority of companies continue deploying the traditional employee personal development plan (PDP): either a matrix excessively weighted to business profit performance, or a mythical document that forms part of a recruiting spiel, never to be seen again.

You need to create a different mindset among your people for dealing with change, so why not take a different approach based on trust through knowledge, data and information:

1. Create a talent acquisition strategy that's best for your business, one that brings reasonable certainty that you will have the right person with the right skills in the right job. Have flexibility, to allow skills to enter the building that you hadn't even thought of.

2. Use your real-time data to build appropriate business performance measurement processes; don't use something out of the archives (even from last year!). You know what is working and what is not, what is profitable and what is not, and what is growing and what is not. Don't over-engineer it.

3. Based on your horizon view, put in place a system where your people are responsible for originating their own personal development, one that is solving problems they think you aren't even aware of yet.

As a leader, promoting all three of the above as a starting point for people development promotes an 'intrapreneurial' culture, one of self-sufficiency and self-promotion. Remember that the pace of change will never be this slow again, and so that you can deal with whatever is thrown at you in life and in business you want support around you not behind you.

In a traditional generic business environment, financial metrics dominate a business-facing PDP with minimal focus on development or training. This is a master–servant situation, where ultimately if the people don't deliver the numbers they are managed sideways, elsewhere or out, or they will make the decision to jump.

In the innovative people-centric PDP scenario we co-create what success looks like for the individual. We appreciate their skill fit, we acknowledge their skill gap, and we commit to what we will provide for them, what we will support them with, and what we will expose them to. If they don't engage in the personal development opportunity then they can be managed sideways, elsewhere, or out.

The performance outcome is usually similar in each scenario, however a people-centric approach irrespective of an individual's personal outcome will build a more sustainable, collaborative, performance-based culture. Okay, so some won't engage, and they will fall away, but it won't detract from the positives around authentic and innovative personal development and opportunity. This creates momentum and builds critical mass around a group of enablers.

One approach promotes a culture of personal improvement leading to business improvement, whereas the other is a management tool for individualising business financial metrics.

You know what is coming when you start a sentence 'with all due respect ... ', however with all due respect ... I believe the traditional Human Resources Manager (HRM) and their internally-facing recruit and report predisposition will become a thing of the past, if it isn't already. Maybe it will change to become more of a facilitation rather than governance process?

SELF-LEADERSHIP

Should you decide you want to be a leader – whether you have been selected to or not – your apprenticeship as a great follower can provide the foundation for that step. However, the risk in this or any transition is that you have not learned how to lead *yourself* first. An even greater risk is that you have not had any learning or development at all.

Before you can lead others, you will need to lead yourself. While we are stepping into a more philosophical space here, it is important to see the wood *and* the trees. This mindset will open you up to the next level of leadership learning.

Here are **six insights that can underpin your leadership style**:

1. **Manage thoughts.** Beware the manifestation of negative thought ... remember, as you think, as you are, and as you remain.

2. **Take initiative.** Don't wait to be asked. Or told.

3. **Prioritise effective.** Busy isn't effective. Cut out the good for the great.

4. **Be authentic.** Let go of needing affirmation and praise.

5. **Bring it on.** By opening your mind to better thinking and doing, you create a capacity for new information.

6. **Personal growth.** Leaders set targets and prioritise personal growth both mentally and physically.

In business, how often are the great workers 'promoted' to managers based on their operational performance only, yet are expected to lead teams of people with various capability, delivering ever-increasing output and managing complex business units for example? Without leadership experience, there is a real possibility the current stakeholder group will become disillusioned by a lack of appropriate interpersonal skills or specific capability required to lead a high-functioning team.

The majority of us want to be part of a success story, and in terms of our impending leadership and the style we will lead with, we need to paint a picture of what winning looks like for us first before we understand what sits behind our how. We need to paint a cognitive picture of how we will optimise and maximise our development and performance.

The **five internal queries that will define your leadership style** are:

1. **My impact.** What does it mean personally to make a difference?

2. **My values.** What are my values and how do they align, or not, with those of the organisation?

3. **My capability.** What is the most effective way to engage, mobilise and sustain people support and effort?

4. **My approach.** What is my method for overcoming obstacles and diffusing problems?

5. **My reaction.** How will I deal with failure? And with success?

The biggest mistake you can make is creating responses or behaviours that you believe are the best fit for your organisation, rather than for yourself first. These are fundamental responses to, and impacts on, an organisation's culture. Who's to say that the organisation has it right? Be prepared to put yourself out there in an environment controlled subtly through both internal and external mentors and a trusted network of feedback.

This is also the type of enquiry framework experienced leaders are recommended to embrace at whatever that relevant point is in their leadership journey.

Authentic reflection and insight as to what moves your leadership needle and where you need to take your ongoing professional development next will ensure your next leadership phase is meaningful at an individual level and successful at an organisational level. The following illustration is a simple method for plotting where you and your success and learnings have come from, and what success could really look like for you personally.

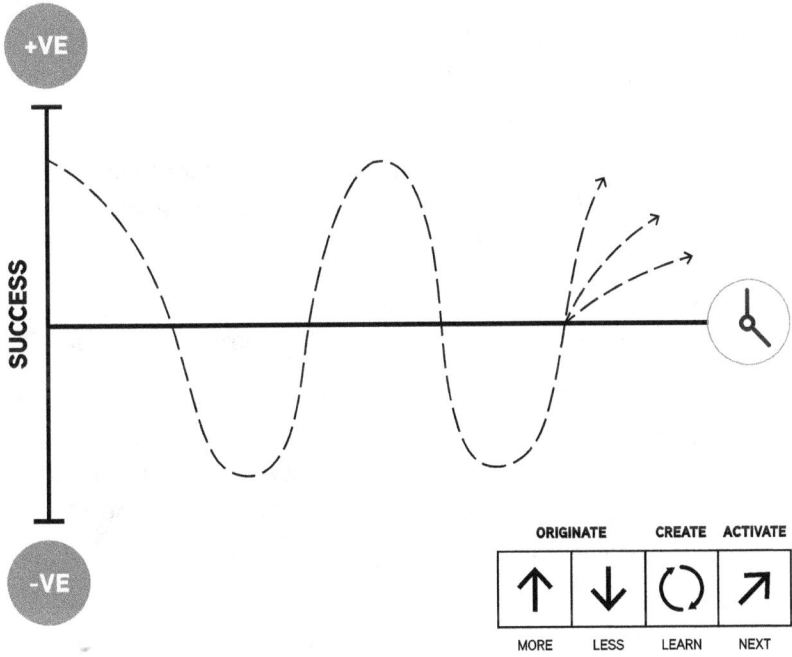

Figure 12. Getting to *next*
Knowing where you best give and receive value will define where you can optimise your best fit. What do you need to do more of, do less of, learn about, and where will that land you next? What do you start, stop and keep?

YOUR MINDSHIFT:
Thinking and doing leadership differently

1. **Be visible.**
   Sitting behind a desk is a very dangerous place from which to lead a business.

2. **Be an exemplar.**
   A high-performing team is simply a management cliché without individual determination, perseverance and persistence led by example.

3. **Can, know and want.**
   Before you can lead others, you must be prepared to lead yourself.

4. **Delegate.**
   Successful leaders seize the opportunity to create the next level of emerging leader, distributed at all levels of the organisation.

5. **You do you.**
   The biggest mistake you can make is creating responses or behaviours that you believe are the best fit for an organisation, rather than for yourself first.

6. **Be authentic.**
   Reflection and insight will ensure your next leadership phase is meaningful at your individual level and successful at an organisational level.

7. **Form a coalition.**
   With the ability to collect, manage and respond to data, bring your colleagues into important conversations.

8. **Learn stuff.**

   An augmented leader is one who has the capability to leverage technology to make fast, sophisticated, data-driven decisions through partnership networks, rather than through chains of command.

9. **Influence culture.**

   Ensure that augmentation and technology do not erode the culture that underpins your business's collective purpose.

10. **Your obligation.**

    Great people are developed by great leaders. It doesn't just happen.

SIX

CASH IS KING

THIS IS NOT ABOUT TURNOVER, IT'S ABOUT WHAT'S LEFT OVER

In a perfect world, board members, executives and business owners shouldn't have any reason to doubt whether or not they can rely on 'the numbers'.

The extent of regulation and governance around financial reporting is voluminous. But the integrity of the numbers can be immediately 'undone' by short-sighted decision-making. By this I mean manipulating decisions around operating assumptions that affect 'the numbers' in an effort to achieve better short-term results. While we hope this may be the exception rather than the rule, it is often the accrued revenues, the forecast margins and aspirational cost management that become the most destructive.

It is amazing really the number of people who can capably count revenue yet cannot manage costs, and believe that profit equals cashflow. In many organisations this translates into an inability to retain and optimise revenue when your ability to earn it is compromised. Quite often there is nothing left over.

In this chapter we look at financial management from a risk-mitigation perspective. We not only look at strategies to stop the bleeding and restore sustainability, but also longer term strategies that will optimise information to enable proactive decision-making and to enforce appropriate governance.

Again, this is all about people being your ultimate enablers. And unfortunately, from a financial perspective, your potential disablers. With the wrong people and processes you will receive the wrong result.

Through my own recruiting mistakes I endured a few false starts, however I was fortunate to have a commercially focused and analytical CFO who was a great scenario modeller – something I'm sure I drove him nuts with. Nonetheless, this was a key success factor in the APM turnaround story.

GATHERING ROCK-SOLID NUMBERS

Rock-solid numbers are the tip of the iceberg in relation to an organisation's vital signs, and the first of the critical interventions that experienced leaders deploy when managing a crisis.

The numbers should also be top of mind for business as usual.

Rock-solid numbers give you guidance so that if (or *when*) something comes out of left field, you know the critical metrics and you know your options, creating greater agility in your response. All too often we hear of business leaders blindsided by what turns out to be poor information, illogical forecasting and inaccurate reporting, leading to profit writedowns, depleted cashflows and, often, a precarious business.

Financial outcomes are the ultimate *effect* and people, including our customers, are the ultimate *cause*. As a leader, forget about blaming the people you empower and engage with; what are *you* doing about this? The buck stops with you.

Consider the following strategies **to get on top of the numbers that matter**:

1. **Key metrics.** Establish your own dashboard of the fundamental, high-level operational KPIs so you can gauge real-time performance.
    *   Have a sense for, say, daily, weekly or monthly cash-based metrics and productivity outcomes that will enable you to accept, question or dig deeper into management reporting.

- It can be as simple as five 'live' numbers that are delivered to you so you can interpret them for net cashflow, overhead liability, breakeven sales, productivity metrics and contingency funds, to name but a few. They need to be the metrics that represent daily business sustainability.

- The critical difference is that *you* interpret the data outside of traditional operational reporting, *you* ask the questions without absolute reliance on complex and colourful spreadsheets, and *you* therefore gain the truly deep insights that *you* need to be able to reliably make fundamental business decisions.

2. **Sensitivity.** Insist on predetermined, consistently applied cashflow variances and sensitivities.

   - Not only does this continuously test your operational forecasts, it allows you to plan differently or to have initiatives that provide, as an example, three scenarios against the top five key risk and opportunity variables.

   - This is not about generating additional and confusingly concurrent strategies, but rather a trigger point from which interventions are deployed from your 'worst case', 'likely case' and 'best case' scenarios.

   - The importance of this is made more relevant due to the volatility, uncertainty, complexity and ambiguity of the new 'business as usual', both in recent years and in particular after the worldwide COVID-19 lockdowns that have shaken global economies to their foundations.

   - As a leader, you will not know everything and that's okay; however, if you can move up a gear into this level of detail, you will be more successful and you will gain credibility through delivering predictable and reliable results.

- Remember, it's about critical numbers, your options, and your response.

3. **Governance.** Beware the reliance on complex, overly detailed and colourful operational reports.

   - The message here is to ensure that any data delivered to you is relevant, current and based on tangible productivity output rather than aspirational forecasts and accruals; that is, you can measure it and you can sense test it. Constantly test data integrity.

   - I believe that traffic light assessments are not your friend. In fact, I am adamant that in crisis management amber does not exist. Either it's high risk or low risk, nothing in between, which provides a very clear method for prioritising resolution. It's go or no-go, not *maybe*.

In amongst our day-to-day operational grind, we need to avoid becoming a database simply collating operational numbers. We don't want to disengage our direct reports through micromanagement, however we do need to find a way to get to succinct, reliable and relevant reporting.

* * *

In a subsequent chapter we discuss from a people perspective an aggressive turnaround strategy I was forced to enact in a business in which I was not only CEO but also one of the major shareholders.

Here is the financial risk management perspective on this.

When crisis unfolds, it actually *unloads*. It just keeps coming.

I had just returned from a trip to the Middle East where I was negotiating a potential relationship with Leighton Contractors;

it was the financial capability seed I needed to plant and grow the business beyond its current $100M revenue capacity.

While I focused on partnership and growth strategies, I entrusted the daily business operations to a stable and seemingly capable ex-tier 1 project manager, whose governance and reporting experience, people network and subcontractor relationships were expected to help prepare us to step up to that next level of business.

I should have entrusted it to my CFO.

One day we sat down and went through the project status report, a financial project-by-project assessment. As a leadership team we had been acting on this format for about six months. The one-line project financials, the traffic light assessment of margin risk, the cashflow graph – you get the picture.

Perhaps it was complacency that caused me to take six months to query the formula behind the project-specific metrics, however I was astounded to learn that it was a forecast based on arbitrary rates of profit *that hadn't been achieved for three years* and *yet-to-be-committed* future costs. Not only was it inaccurate, it was bordering on dishonest, if not for the genuinely delusional thinking behind it.

Needless to say, the formula was immediately stripped back to reality, less a contingency, and every project forecast profit fell into the red traffic light zone and nearly every project cashflow graph flatlined at best. Sobering is an understatement when you have just wiped $3M off your bottom line. This is when I realised we would be contracting $100M worth of high-risk, single-figure margin construction for a nett nil outcome that year.

This discovery and realisation were a week before I received that business-defining call from an insolvency practitioner alleging that my business was indebted $9M to his client. Disruption was headed our way.

ATTACKING THE COST BASE

While an uncertain economic environment requires the lean approach, we need to ask whether we are cost cutting to temporarily inflate the bottom line and hoping to improve cashflow, or are we restructuring to regenerate the business?

And at what point should this intervention be introduced?

Restructuring is a pre-planned initiative to optimise and maximise current resources to meet the current and anticipated market, whereas cost cutting is simply stopping the bleeding ... for now. Both are relevant at a specific point in time.

Either way, how do we know we are 'restructuring' the right areas, in the right sequence, with the right people, for the optimum outcome?

Attacking the cost base via a systematic, planned assessment of the business's overheads will be one of the actions of a Tactical Response Plan's financial objective. A successful business is adaptable in terms of systems and processes, and agile in terms of cost structure. Here's what you need to do:

1. **Analyse fixed costs.** Break down the overhead component and/or specific business unit into accountable expense lines for a detailed assessment.

   - Too often, we start with an assessment of people – roles, responsibilities and remuneration – which is not always the right answer. You must undertake a quantitative analysis of each resource and the impact they have in generating, managing and/or supporting revenue-generating activities.

- Drill into the fixed costs first – not only does this allow you to assess, for example, outsourcing opportunities, it will also generate some quick wins and show the business that it's not just people being restructured. Thus, the purpose of the restructure will gain credibility.

2. **Value add.** Identify the synergies, integration and outsourcing opportunities, and remove the duplications.

   - What are the administrative and/or related tasks that can be managed by external specialists? Well-entrenched, historical systems and processes are usually indicative of a business that is reluctant to meet volatility and uncertainty head on.

   - Identifying synergies through integrating specific functions common to different business units often provides a quick win and another level of people engagement through diversification of roles and responsibilities.

   - Do you know what part technology can play inside the back office of your business? New problems are being solved every day through easy to source, cloud-based apps and technologies, not to mention the data that generates real-time business analytics, plus the benefits of a more people-efficient overhead structure.

3. **Forecast.** Don't just target costs inside the Profit & Loss – rationalising future liabilities can also create an opportunity to be more agile and receptive to alternate strategies.

   - Divesting underperforming operations is a no-brainer, however beware those who won't ask the tough questions around operations that may hold some historical, rather than commercial, value. An example of 'holding on' to eventually fail.

- While bricks and mortar have long been held as a fundamental foundation to any balance sheet, have you assessed the cost/benefit in divesting part, or all, of the asset, and then investing the capital in 'bigger picture' business growth via outsourcing, partnership or technology? What strategy will create the longer term benefit?

- Attacking your cost base leads to the ultimate goal of any lean business: having engaged an efficient level of capable resources to deliver the optimum return measured by secured market share, sustainable bottom line, and prospects for continued growth.

Here are **five fundamental cost management questions to ask yourself**:

1. **Are we lean and mean?** If I am cost cutting to stop the bleeding, what is my end game? What needs to happen by when for the bleeding stop?

2. **What is our end game?** And to what extent am I restructuring the cost base to sustain our compelling reason for being in business? To what extent will our purpose be impacted?

3. **Have we retained capability?** How do I know I am restructuring the right areas, in the right sequence, with the right people, for the optimum outcome?

4. **How invested are our partners?** What is my supply chain partnership strategy?

5. **Where is our financial parachute?** What does my cash buffer look like and how do I access external capital? Is it debt or is it equity?

OPTIMISING FINANCE AND RISK STRUCTURES

The reason we refer to 'structures' is this is all about the 'how' – from both an internal and external perspective.

Your ability to be agile and to quickly respond to any crisis from a financial perspective is dependent upon having robust, efficient and accurate internal disciplines that provide you with the ability to extract real-time support from your external finance and risk stakeholders.

If you can't meet external processes with your internal governance, you may be wasting your time. And this can't be reactionary – you must be ready to 'go' at all times.

When it comes to managing finance and risk structures, the effectiveness of your internal commercial discipline and the integrity of your external stakeholder relationships will be your game changers. How relevant are your internal processes? Have you delegated responsibilities that will commit the business to risk? Are you a 'tick the box' organisation or an agile, collaborative democracy of decision-makers?

To map out a process improvement pathway, I suggest you start with the following look in the rear-view mirror, as a potential way forward:

1. **Delegations.** Do you have a document that clearly delegates responsibility and authority on behalf of the company? Is this responsibility and authority reviewed annually? If you assessed it right now, is it relevant today?

2. **History.** What previous financial issues have negatively impacted the business and what could have been done to mitigate them?

3. **Risk and opportunity.** What opportunities have we missed out on or lost because we were unprepared or slow to react, and how could we compliantly fast-track this next time?

4. **Roadblocks.** What has been the most significant impediment in terms of operational inertia? From an internal productivity perspective, where can we optimise and maximise without compromise?

5. **Digital disruption.** What impact does, and will, technology have on our commercial disciplines? Are we current and relevant in terms of technology?

As a business leader, you will know the external deals and their commercial obligations, and you will know the 'what' from an operational perspective. But is the risk assessment process commercially, contractually and productively effective? Does it add value?

When the screws are tightening, having all your financial and risk relationships in one basket may deny you the opportunity of deploying the 'other parachute' if and when you need it.

Rather than a 'set and forget' relationship with your financial partners, maintaining regular, personal, face-to-face dialogue with them will allow you to wedge their door open at the times when you really need them.

Consider the following:

1. **Diversification.** Diversification and/or syndication to a second tier of professional services will not only maintain ongoing commercially competitive terms, it will also mitigate your reliance on one provider and perhaps only one option.

2. **Debt.** You should always have access to a capital facility, as you may not be able to get it when you need it. When the

macroeconomic screws tighten, the operating cash buffer or opportunity to diversify may be what really moves the needle.

3. **Partners.** Establish relationships that could generate a growth-focused equity interest. It's not about giving up the farm in a time of crisis. Instead, it's about looking for that blue ocean, that expansion or diversification, that may get you to a longer term *next*.

4. **Options.** Have a clear picture of what traditional bank debt looks like, and what the options and alternatives are. Having flexibility and access to short-term alternate capital markets is another 'nice to have', assuming that you've got the bases covered.

Maintaining an almost subconscious current and realistic picture of your key finance and risks relationships will provide you with the best opportunity for informed, urgent and accurate decision-making ahead of time.

It's all about preparedness and being 'battle ready' should that crisis eventuate.

It's about enabling relationships that give you access to the decision-makers that also have a vested interest in keeping your business in front of the game.

TRANSLATING DATA INTO GOOD DECISIONS

The ability to manage huge volumes of data enabling fundamental and timely decision-making is critical to a company's success. It is worthwhile of inclusion in the financial chapter due to the business imperative of raw data producing accurate information.

Data has always been fundamental for companies, however as the amount and usefulness of data has soared through increased storage capacities and processing power in recent years, it has become one of the most important assets in business.

Having technology, human talent and a data-management function is a great start, however this alone will not be effective in the absence of a value-creating strategy for organising, governing, analysing and utilising an organisation's information assets.

Data strategy is a specialist field, however it justifies its importance when proactive leaders and followers can consider what they need to do to be able to leverage the information they have access to. Superior data management and analytics are essential capabilities that support strategic decision-making and, ultimately, business performance optimisation

Much of the information on enterprise data management is technical and focused on compliance and governance, however with the capability its analysis now brings through continuous digital innovation it can now be leveraged more than ever to support a business's overall commercial, rather than just technological, strategy for example.

This evolution in data management requires an understanding of defensive (controlling) strategy, and offensive (enabling) strategy. 'Defensive' refers to building a robust foundation in terms of data integrity, and 'offensive' refers to using data to execute business (customer-centric) objectives. Regardless of whether a heavily regulated insurer (predominantly defensive focusing on compliance) or a clothing retailer (predominantly offensive focusing on e-commerce), best practice data management strategies land on a trade-off between both defensive and offensive.

For example, Amazon is almost entirely a data-driven organisation. Customers receive a personalised experience based on what they, or customers like them, have previously purchased. Its shipping model uses predictive analysis to ensure products suggested to you are located nearby or are easily accessible, which enables quicker delivery times. Delivery costs are kept low by directing products through the cheapest routes. They have a robust platform for storing and keeping private their customer data, and for ensuring a secure payment gateway. They are heavily data offensive, and also appropriately data defensive.

The 'underground infrastructure' of data management may not be as seductive as the predictive analysis models and interactive dashboards they generate, however it is vital to high performance and sustainability.

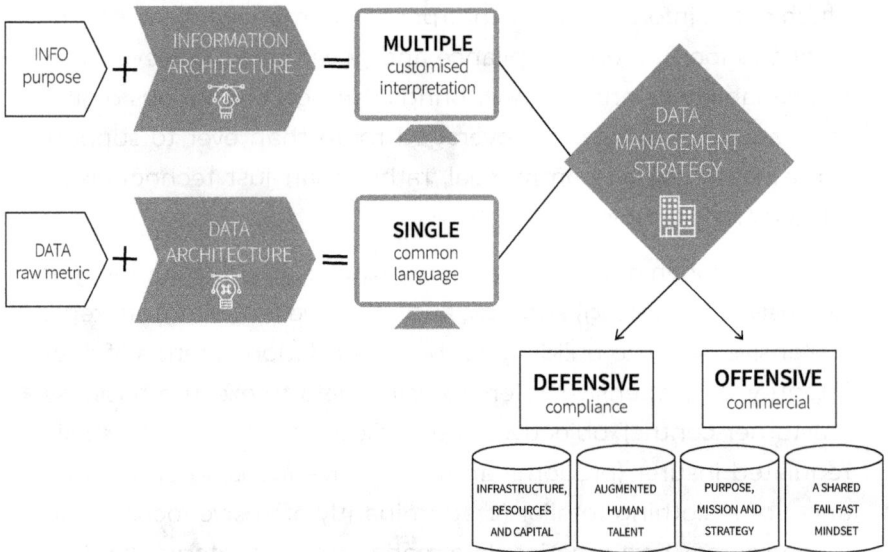

Figure 13. Data management strategy
The trade-off between business-compliance defensive strategies and business-enabling offensive strategies

Here are **seven strategies to optimise a data strategy**:

1. **Connection.** Even if you don't know the full extent yet, link potential data use to each one of your strategic priorities.

2. **Alignment.** What are some quick initiatives that have or can receive change 'buy-in' for a bigger data picture?

3. **Information.** Know your data limit – do you have it all, do you need to create more, or outsource it?

4. **Governance.** Who, how and what will manage data integrity, storage and use? And have a knowledge of General Data Protection Regulations.

5. **Infrastructure.** Do you know what hardware and software you will need?

6. **People.** Do you have the expert skills to deliver your data needs?

7. **Planning.** Engage in structured implementation and change management initiatives.

YOUR MINDSHIFT:
Being all over the numbers

You must look inside and outside of the Profit & Loss statement in order to gain a true financial picture. You must rely on multiple sources of truth that derive from:

1. **Forecasts.**
   It is the human error or the assumptions around accrued revenues, margin calculations and aspirational cost management strategies that will cause the greatest financial destruction.

2. **Financial acumen.**
   With wrong people and flawed processes you will receive the wrong result. Commercially focused analytical financial skills far outweigh operational know-how and bean-counting.

3. **Information.**
   Establish your own dashboard of the fundamental high-level operational KPIs so that you can gauge real-time performance. Do not simply make a P&L data selection.

4. **Sensitivity.**
   Within your key metrics, insist on predetermined, consistently applied cashflow variances and sensitivities. Remember, it's about critical operational numbers, your options, and your response.

5. **Governance.**
   Beware the complex, overly detailed and colourful operational report and the true data it may disguise. Traffic lights are designed to manage vehicle flow, not cashflow.

6. **Rationalising.**

   Whether it be cost cutting to stop the bleeding, or restructuring to create efficiency, do you know if you are rationalising the right areas, in the right sequence, with the right people, for the optimum outcome?

7. **Synergies.**

   Be prepared to move away from traditional doing. Identify the overlaps and remove duplications. Look at overhead integration and outsourcing opportunities.

8. **Fixed costs.**

   Too often we forget about or are not prepared to commit to the effort involved in undoing fixed costs or restructuring fixed assets, which is usually short-term pain for long-term gain.

9. **Suppliers.**

   Have a win–win strategy so that your creditor liabilities are manageable and you have a certainty in future supply chain relationships. This will be unique to them if it is strategic rather than transactional.

10. **Partners.**

    Maintaining regular face-to-face dialogue with institutional finance and risk partners, and debtors, will allow you to wedge their door open at the times when you really need them.

SEVEN

EXPONENTIAL BUSINESS

ROLLING THE DICE ON CHANGE

When we talk about exponential business, we refer to the value it creates. To produce exponential value we must create a shift from an *incremental* mindset that will make something better to an *exponential* mindset that will make something different, and better, evolving quicker.

Incremental is linear – immediate and steady, whereas exponential is accumulating and accelerating. This is the paradigm shift between business models built on industrial machinery to business models that now leverage technology.

Let's consider the financial crisis brought about by the COVID-19 pandemic, and three fundamental business outcomes – to take a dive, survive, or thrive:

- One option is to **terminate**. To shut up shop, to get out. You've had enough.

- Another option is to **hibernate**, to lay low. To batten down the hatches, weather the storm and see it through to the other side, ready to go again. But beware short-term survival at the expense of long-term sustainability, as to hibernate in this period of disruption at such scale, you may actually come out so far behind that incremental may not even 'cut it'.

- The game-changing option is to **innovate**. To use the current crisis as a means to find a different way of thinking and doing. To leverage uncertainty, roadblocks and bottlenecks into a new offering, a point of difference that solves new problems. This is the exponential mindset that unlocks future value.

In this chapter we consider the cognitive mindset as well as the tangible resources that will be the precursor to successful change.

Choose *what* to change before choosing *how*

The academic research is really clear that when corporations launch transformations, roughly 70% fail.[1] Corporate transformations have a tragic success rate – they can be:

1. incorrectly diagnosed, producing irrelevant strategies

2. poorly implemented and fail to deliver the anticipated results

3. sidelined

4. abandoned entirely.

From a business perspective we cannot *not* have change during an unprecedented period of acceleration, innovation and disruption. It is a very quick and easy process to become a statistic if you don't respond.

Flawed implementation is most often blamed for failure, the people, leadership and strategy drivers of which we have discussed extensively. But poor execution is only part of the problem; experience suggests that especially in complex and fast-moving environments, hasty and misguided decisions about *how to transform* to remain competitive are made, leading to an unrealistic effort to stay in front of the game.

Often organisations pursue the wrong changes.

Before worrying about *how* to change, businesses need to figure out *what* to change and, in particular, what to change *first*. They must choose their change management battles wisely as their endeavours could have a negative impact on not only commercial performance but also the engagement and effort of their people, increasing exponentially the likelihood of new problems.

---

1   McKinsey & Company. 'Why Do Most Transformations Fail?' Online. July 2019.

Visionary leaders will collaborate, seek counsel and immerse themselves in their business, their customers and their people, so as to answer the following **five organisational change health check queries**:

1. **Disruption.** What disruptions are we facing, and what disruptions can we create?

2. **Sustainability.** Are we willing to look at future business from a need rather than want perspective, or are we stuck in time?

3. **Distraction.** What are the potential roadblocks or solutions that the current and future business environment will provide?

4. **Purpose.** From where does the business's core success and value originate, and to what extent are we now diverging from this? Are we at odds with our fundamental reason for being?

5. **Capability.** Do we have capable people who can, know and want to be part of a shift, and do we have access to the resources that will enable this?

HORIZON PLANNING

Digging deeper into the previous concepts of irrelevant business models, complacency and delusion – those scenarios that we describe as 'holding on' strategies destined to fail – is where some organisations will give up and allow innovation to give way to inertia.

Some businesses are reluctant to believe they have a finite lifetime, that they have 'always done it this way' and cannot see beyond their current existence. To achieve growth and a sustainable existence throughout their corporate lifetime, organisations must optimise existing businesses while creating opportunities for emerging or new opportunities. Innovative businesses refer to 'portfolio terms' or 'product life' or 'project period', for example, as the timeframe that defines their current existence.

McKinsey's original Three Horizons Model, often referenced as a foundation for innovation strategy, is very prescriptive in terms of innovation timeframes and a structured progression through (1) core business, then (2) emerging opportunities, leading to (3) profitable new business.[2]

However, in today's fast-paced commercial world, the horizons within which you need to operate are considerably more fluid than that, dependent upon such factors as globalisation, competition, regulation, innovation, expertise and technology, for example – none of which operate to finite timelines or prearranged expiry dates.

It is the agile businesses that predict their horizon ahead of time, that are already looking for ways to innovate and capitalise current propositions before they are forced to.

It's unlikely you will pinpoint exactly your horizon transition date – and it's pointless attempting to. However, with the ability now to access considerable volumes of real-time data, you will have a very clear picture of what needs to change by when. And there needs to be an overlap period, a critical pre-planned point from which transformation can be managed.

---

2   Baghai, M., White, D. and Coley, S. *The Alchemy of Growth*. 2000.

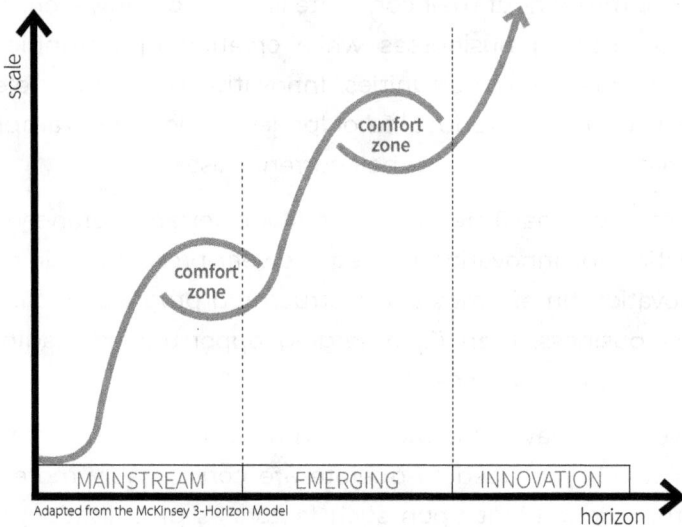

Figure 14. The three horizons

A continuous evolution through mainstream, emerging and innovative business modelling

THE TRANSITION TO EXPONENTIAL

PROFILE	HORIZON 1	HORIZON 2	HORIZON 3
MAINSTREAM	dominant	declining	buffer
EMERGING	active	developing	dominant
INNOVATION	research	modelling	active

Figure 15. Horizon shift

The various scales of 'next level' transitioning where innovation leaves behind the concept of infinite business modelling

Consider these **five methods to qualify and quantify your horizon**:

1. **Market intelligence.** Use your product ecosystem feedback loop.

2. **Direct enquiry.** Ask the customer, what do you need next?

3. **Expert prediction.** Constructed consensus on the basis of specific enquiry.

4. **Trend analysis.** Extrapolate historical data into the future.

5. **Internal assessment.** SWOT analysis, particularly weaknesses and threats.

DON'T JUST CHANGE, MAKE IT FUNDAMENTALLY DIFFERENT

In today's dynamic business environment there isn't one management style that's consistently effective, rather a responsive approach to stay ahead, one that requires leaders to understand how and when to deploy different leadership styles.

Industry-changing companies across the spectrum of business models are thriving on exponential thinking that enables experimentation, continuous improvement, and growth. While mindset is the enabler or *the how*, technology is quite often *the what*.

In chapter 5 we compared fixed and growth mindsets. From a much broader organisation-wide leadership perspective there is room to consider the concept of shared mindsets – one that considers a collective mobilising of mindsets, a much larger scale of numerous and complex perspectives creating a picture of what success could look like exponentially, allowing individuals responsible for future growth to thrive in an uncertain future. To 'go for it'.

Harnessing the power of technology is an important part of driving transformation and future growth, the innovation and reinvention that we all now refer to. (It's important to mention that by technology we refer simply to that which is readily available to all organisations – from integrated management systems to the gig economy, for example.)

To make that quantum leap from incremental improvement to exponential growth can be frightening, however it is the shared mindset of what success could look like that will enable that leap. We need to trust it, made easier by the fact that we know where we will end up if we don't. And remember that 'fail fast and move on' is a considerably more exponential mindset as opposed to doing nothing, which in reality could mean that you are going backwards even faster!

Assuming exponential transformation 'just happens' is delusional.

Successful transformations will produce the right organisational mindset and culture, starting with acknowledging the gap from incremental to exponential, committing to 'unlearning' ingrained and outdated management practices, and of course 'learning' new ways of thinking and doing.

The scope and scale of an organisation-specific transformation depends upon such variables as the industry it participates in, the sectors within it, the macro and micro economy informing it, and the point within a product or service's life cycle.

Consider the following **five foundation transformations from which to build your own burning platform for change**:

1. **Strategy transformation** powers an organisation's growth engine. It is the compelling story, the 'different thinking' that will get a business to its *next* through market-leading

differentiation, through using data and experience to predict trends, to solve problems that don't exist yet.

2. **Business model transformation** is the 'different doing' that comes from the different thinking brought about by strategy transformation. This spectrum runs from a change in the customer-facing commercial proposition to a change in the metrics a company uses to track performance. Ultimately, it is the continuum under which a business will rewrite its competitive playbook.

3. **Operational transformation** is simply doing core business better, faster or cheaper. While this doesn't have to specifically be digital, in a rapidly changing world operational change is what will ensure cost efficiency and, ultimately, sustainability. Sure, we might have a unique strategy in a blue ocean of opportunity, however it will only be a matter of time before we will be yesterday's news without a mindset of doing better with same, or more with less.

4. **People transformation** is not only enhancing the culture within which people will optimise performance, it is a mindset of incentivising future capability. It is a forward-looking approach to building the competency bridge between the organisation's *what now* and *what's next*. The critical success factor here is acknowledging that the definition of people starts with the top, and it extends outside.

5. **Performance transformation** is quite simply the efficiency gain through the sum of all of the parts. It's connecting all of the components and capability that will maximise a commercial, environmental and societal impact, for example. It is the measure by which a compelling business proposition will be sustained, or not.

Unless you are a start-up with a proven minimum viable product and exponential is your only way to the top, fast, it is important for existing businesses going through this transformation to acknowledge the stability that retaining some incremental 'business as usual' thinking will bring. You will need cashflow to procure exponential technology and people, and you will need 'business as usual' as the platform to shift your customers, your people and your offering.

While exponential thinking is needed to realise 10× future growth, incremental thinking may just retain or bring surety to, say, 10% of your viability while you get there. And both will co-exist in an exponential enterprise.

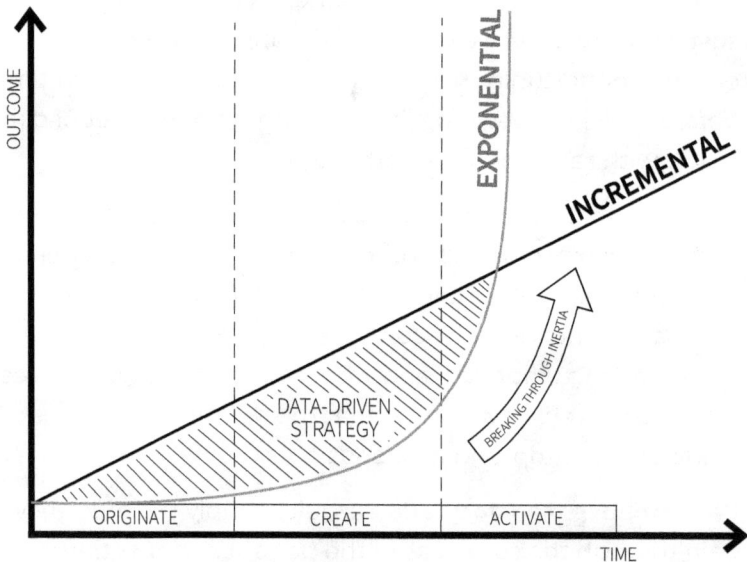

Figure 16. Exponential outcomes
Outcomes obtained through data-driven strategic sensing, thinking and doing, despite the initial drag of an organisation's inertia

In 1923 Walt Disney created an animated storytelling entertainment business, made successful through that early phase right through to the 1930s with classics we all know that included *Snow White and the Seven Dwarfs*, *Cinderella*, *Pinocchio* and *Dumbo*.

Thereafter followed 50 years of moderate success expanding the business across film, entertainment and amusement, before some considerable success in the late 1980s and '90s with animated movies such as *The Little Mermaid*, *Beauty and the Beast*, *The Lion King* and *Aladdin*.

There was a period from the mid 1990s when Disney struggled or was only moderately successful, no doubt impacted by the disruption brought about by digital alternatives such as Blockbuster, a provider of home movie and video game rental services that expanded internationally at that time (and was disrupted itself some time later by Netflix and others).

When Bob Iger became CEO of Disney in 2005, his picture of success was framed around the fact that when Disney produced great animation the business was extremely successful. However, the best animation people and leadership was within the Steve Jobs majority owned Pixar Studios. This was a business Disney had a previous co-funding and co-production relationship with, from which Steve Jobs enacted a famous public divorce in 2004 citing irreconcilable differences around creative and contract disputes.

While the Pixar relationship seemed irreparable, Bob Iger saw that Pixar's great storytellers, artists, technology, brand and original stories along with a great Disney legacy was ultimately what success looked like for Disney. This was his exponential move, to turnaround the Disney organisation using the business model that was the foundation of its original success almost 100 years earlier: animation.

Despite opening the door to discussions with Disney's new CEO, Steve Jobs – adamant that a culture of creativity was Pixar's value creator – was concerned that Disney's one-dimensional proposition would destroy Pixar.

Two years of relationship rebuilding, a commitment by Disney to co-create with rather than dominate Pixar, and strategic alignment around creating original stories rather than relying on historical fairy tales enabled a negotiation that saw Disney acquire Pixar for $7.4B in 2006.

Over 12 years, Disney's shift from incremental to exponential under Bob Iger saw Disney become a fully diversified, direct-to-consumer, multi-channel proposition, now called Disney+, having invested more than $70B acquiring Pixar, Marvel Studios, Lucas Films and 20th Century Fox.

Iger saw the damage that protecting the traditional Disney brand was doing to the business. However, by respecting the Disney brand through innovation, he allowed it to evolve into a $100B+ multi-disciplined sustainable entertainment business.

An interesting footnote to the strategy alignment was Bob Iger's insistence for the new Disney Pixar business to continue to show empowered young women with a purpose, as was illustrated in the *Snow White*, *Cinderella* and *Sleeping Beauty* originals. Pixar obliged by flipping the main character gender in sequels such as *Incredibles 2* and *Finding Dory*, and later, the new Captain Marvel was female (and the movie grossed more than $1B globally). A great example of leading with meaning and purpose.

YOUR MINDSHIFT:
Be prepared to rewrite the rules

1. **Business is a game.**
   It is won or lost on the back of strategies to survive, played within a set of dynamic rules executed with varying levels of skill by numerous participants.

2. **Don't be left behind.**
   From a business perspective we can't *not* have change during an unprecedented period of acceleration, innovation and disruption. It is quick and easy to become yesterday's news.

3. **Change is the new normal.**
   Change will never be this slow again.

4. **Have a game plan.**
   Before worrying about how to change, you need to figure out what to change, and in particular what to change first.

5. **Collective thinking.**
   A much broader leadership perspective will enable shared mindsets to create a much larger scale of complex ideas and numerous iterations of what winning looks like.

6. **Break it to fix it.**
   Be willing to look at future business from a need rather than want perspective, as opposed to being stuck in time protecting history.

7. **Don't hibernate.**
   It is an exponential mindset that looks at risk as opportunity and ultimately unlocks future value. Gone are the days of just being able to ride it out.

8. **Horizon planning.**
   Every business has a finite lifetime to some degree.
   Successful and sustainable businesses are already looking
   for ways to innovate and capitalise business as usual.

9. **Think and do differently.**
   Innovation is not so much producing technology, it is the
   process of thinking and doing differently that will lead you
   to whatever technology or tool best leverages disruption.

10. **Disrupt yourself.**
    Be curious – learning and experiencing something different,
    and being uncomfortable at times in that, is vital for
    innovation and building instinct for what *next* might look
    like. Unfortunately, it is rarely an epiphany.

EIGHT

START WITH THE
END IN MIND

DON'T MAKE IT UP AS YOU GO

Organisations that can respond and adapt to a changing and turbulent economic environment are the ones most likely to prosper. Those that cannot or do not adapt simply won't.

In fear of stating the obvious, the business environment within which we operate is in a constant state of flux, brought about by aggressive macroeconomic conditions in a hyper-connected global marketplace, accelerated by technology. There is a lot going on.

Whatever the cause, the effects are the same across all industries and sectors. The frenetic pace of change, and the urgency required to respond, makes each challenge more significant from a leadership perspective. When it comes to business transformation, the one certainty about the future is the pace of change will only accelerate.

Developing a sustainable business over the long term has therefore never been more of a test. As a leader of a business, an organisation or a community, you need to be ready for the incoming challenges, regardless of whether you have a crisis right now or you are aware that preparation for the sudden onset of one will not be an opportunity lost.

The scrutiny on investment and expenditure.

The interrogation of risk assessments.

The continual restructuring of financial arrangements.

The willingness of clients to chase the cheapest price.

The continuing threat of substitutes in an increasingly competitive marketplace.

The evolution of a tech-savvy and comfortably transient workforce.

These are only a *few* of the factors boiling away in a much larger pressure cooker of operating variables, and this environment requires business leaders to leave behind historical management practices and embrace a mindset of regular reinvention in order to capitalise on a dynamic and global business environment.

A leader without a compelling business story creating new opportunities out of current threats is simply a manager with a delusional plan, often simply adding 10% to last year's Profit & Loss and calling it strategy.

In this chapter I continue to promote the concept that strategy is a demonstration of leadership *how*. The two are inextricably linked, through forward-thinking a way to a sustainable *next*. I refrain from discussing the academics of strategy philosophy, however we do discuss the cognitive imperatives that are often assumed, taken for granted or perhaps not even top of mind.

Let's start by looking at your purpose, mission, strategy and values.

Your reason for being:

Purpose is why you do what you do. It is your compelling story, a clear statement that describes the benefit of your offer, how you solve your customer's needs, and what distinguishes you from the competition.

Vision is the 'pie in the sky', your aspirational bigger picture.

Mission is what you do. It is your method for adding value with internal resources, and it is a second *why*, the one that sits behind your strategy.

Strategy is how you achieve your purpose. It is your implementation plan for optimising and maximising performance.

Values are the enabling behaviours that execute your strategy and mission.

* * *

The concept of co-creation remains foreign to many people who have not considered that in the context of establishing a unique value proposition, designing your methodology for adding value, constructing your implementation plan and building your talent pool to do all of that, the concept of co-creation is the game changer. It is collective seeing, thinking, planning and acting differently – multiple perspectives that generate diverse thought and, potentially, multiple opportunities

The mistake many people make is that they go straight to strategy, and in doing so they overlook 'picking apart' their organisational reason for being. Often the reason this happens is that these people are toiling away in the operational trench, the *what* and the *how*, and they have not understood their need to differentiate through their *why*.

Or perhaps they haven't had exposure to understand that their *why* is in fact a differentiator, or haven't had the prior experience of interrogating a *why* in the first place. And that's okay, because not everyone is born with a '*why* radar'.

In the same vein as the concept of people before profit, when businesses are deliberate about prioritising purpose beyond profit and are effective in how they serve a broad cross-section of societal constituencies – employees, suppliers, vendors and communities – results that favour the bottom line will be a logical outcome.[1]

---

1   Ucuzoglu, J. 'Three Megatrends Could Make Or Break Your Business This Decade.' *Chief Executive*. Online. January 2020.

Here are three simple questions that will commence, and by no means complete, your initial vision and, in turn, that which will inform your *why* thinking:

1. Why do we do what we do?
2. Why are we good at what we do?
3. What do people say about us?

There are many experts who define *why*, who will help you find your *why* and articulate or 'pitch' your *why*, and others will explain how to market your *why* and to commercialise your *why*.

One of those experts who has impacted my strategic sensing fundamentally is Marc Stigter. He is also the author of a number of books, including co-authoring the award-winning *Solving the Strategy Delusion*. To find your compelling story, Marc asks, among other questions:

- To whom will you add value?

- With what kind of services?

- And what are your points of difference?

I have used these questions and various iterations thereof for more than 10 years, and have created a simple framework which will allow succinct and specific responses and the ability to artic-ulate your *why*, shown on the following page with a hypothetical example.

Your original *what*	We specialise in building apartments. We have been in business for 20 years and turnover $150M per year.
A possible response	So what? So do 100 others.

YOUR VALUE EQUATION = YOUR COMPELLING *WHY*

YOUR ENQUIRY	YOUR IMPACT
1. Where have we come from?	• Design and construct builder • Profitable contractor with nil debt
2. To whom do we add value?	• Institutional superannuation funds • High-net-worth family offices
3. What kind of services?	• Design and construction • Project funding • Research and development
4. What are our points of difference?	• Turnkey funding model • Facade manufacturing business • Known industry experts in-house • Financial services business bolt-on
5. Why do we do what we do?	• Design and construction is our core skill • Our cash flows enable a funding product • Funding creates negotiated opportunities • Negotiation removes high-risk tendering and sunk costs • We partner with blue chip clients • We can attract the industry's best people
6. What does our success look like?	• Preferred partner via negotiation • No hard money tender, ever • Funding margin exceeds construction margin • Acquired by multinational corporation within three years

Your bigger picture	To be the only financial services partner in Australasia with turnkey design and construct capability.
Your compelling *why*	To deploy our innovative methods and entrepreneurial models so as to change the industry perception of defect and distress generally; and so as to create negotiated opportunities, sustainable business and financial success specifically.
A meaningful *what*	As a contractor we fund, design and construct projects for major institutional funds and high-net-worth families throughout Australasia. As a manufacturer we own critical timeframes, we reduce production costs and we remove risk.
A likely response	Wow! How do I qualify to negotiate with you?

Figure 17. Value equation

Why you do what you do, assuming that your values have been resolved and are relevant to your why

And just to complete this thought process, a compelling 'elevator pitch' may go something like: 'We are the only contractor in Australia that has the capacity to design, construct, manufacture and finance multiple projects in excess in $100M.' Boom.

Remembering that the above example is generic and has not been co-created, it does however illustrate the transition or shift from 'so what' to 'wow'.

Leading with *why* has a deeper, more emotional and ultimately more influential value.[2]

Fundamentally, what we are trying to achieve is what Kim and Mauborgne refer to as a 'blue ocean', an environment where an uncontested marketplace is created through low cost and differentiation, one where the competition is irrelevant. This is an adaptation of the term 'niche', and is a response to mitigate fierce competition and downward pressure on pricing.

This blue ocean concept is no doubt aspirational, but as an example, how I get my mind to shift to this thinking is not through a mindset of searching for a new business idea per se, but more so by looking for what opportunity lies in the roadblocks and bottlenecks that dominate a specific industry or offering, for example.

(In chapter 9 we put this co-creating mindset into practice through following a 7-Step business transformation process called the MindShift Method.)

WHAT SUCCESS NEEDS TO LOOK LIKE

Unfortunately, we do not live in a perfect world. Alas for some of us perfectionists it can be a difficult concept to grasp, however

---

2   Sinek, S. *Find Your Why*. 2017.

from a transformation perspective you cannot move forward if you ignore why it is you are where you are.

Before you step through the detail and focus of the MindShift Method in chapter 9, it is recommended that you take a collaborative helicopter view first, simply planting the seed and kick-starting the next level of thinking.

You will need to identify your organisation's problems – the downside. Articulate your deep fear or potential maximum fallout should these problems prevail. Keep it simple and don't analyse this to the point of paralysis. It could be as simple (in explanation, that is!) as:

Problem: Market share has reduced 20% year on year

Deep fear Staff exits
Business loss
Market relevance
Sustainability

Or:

Problem: Project losses have absorbed $5M of cash reserves

Deep fear Project legacy issues
Staff exits
Business loss
Insolvency

Acknowledge at a high level the mistakes that have been made, and document them in the centrepiece of your model. (Call them 'challenges' if the concept of mistakes is too raw for you, although if you are going to move forward, it shouldn't be!). They might simplistically include:

- a set-and-forget mentality
- an irrelevant business plan
- outdated technical resources
- a lowest price proposition
- over-reliance on consultants
- poor governance and risk management.

Oscar Wilde famously declared that experience is simply the name we give our mistakes. That works for me.

You will work out by now that next we articulate what success looks like for us. What are your solution(s) – your upside, and therefore, what is the organisation's ultimate prize? It could look something like:

Solution: 30% market share locally, 10% globally

Ultimate prize   Entity value
Employer of choice
Market relevance
Sustainability

Or:

Solution: 10% margins on all projects

Ultimate prize   Repeat business
Balance sheet for growth.
Employer of choice.
Building cash reserves.

What we are doing here is creating a vision for what success needs to look like by shifting current thinking from an isolated view of the problem through a much wider impact, opening up thinking around broader perspectives and ultimately a raft of potential solutions.

On the basis that you already have a cohort of ACE people around you, an anonymous exercise around what is each person's deep fear and ultimate prize will ensure discretionary efforts are genuine, that there is vested interest, and a more complete picture of where you are now and where you need to get to. Should this process also flush out any remote or disengaged behaviours then they weren't on your team in the first place!

This can be a real test for some people; ownership (generally) can be a psychological burden when there are both business risks and personal reputation impacts attached to it.

This initial strategy sensing is also an effective way whereby you or a facilitator or whomever is running this show can receive context. It is not a strategy yet. It is all up for grabs; it simply paints a picture, a picture that I guarantee will change by the time you get to the end of the strategic planning process if there has been authentic and different thinking.

A DRAG RACE TO THE BOTTOM

You don't want to start with this particular end in mind, however there were 10,748 insolvency appointments across Australia in FY2019.[3] In round numbers, that is 900 per month and around 45 per business day. Even without the specific details of the numerous categories, this is an extraordinary statistic that represents approximately 5% of the 236,724 new companies registered in the previous year.[4]

---

3   ASIC Summary Analysis of Insolvency Statistics as at 6 January 2020.
4   Ibid.

Having been close to the edge once upon a time, these types of statistics always provoke deep *what if* thoughts for me:

- How did the business get to this point?
- How many of these appointments followed a disciplined intervention in an attempt to save the business?
- How many of these interventions were led by external experts?
- How many of these appointments were a result of the leadership simply 'holding on' to business as usual, waiting for it to improve?
- What was the real cost in terms of both direct and indirect financial loss, of future business opportunity lost, and the personal impact on physical and mental health?

It is not uncommon for businesses to go it alone and undertake their own transformation according to their inside-out view of what success needs to look like. Others may engage an expert and then take over implementation because they know best ... forgetting why they are where they are! And others may simply commence but not complete, because their similarly internal view informs them that the world has changed and they now have it covered.

Delusional, to say the least.

Okay, this may be a cynical view and it could be the exception and not the rule, but why not do it once, do it right and do it completely, to the point of reinvention?

Obviously, this is all about co-creating a unique and compelling strategy, however the success or not of any stage of any intervention sends a very clear message as to what success looks like for those around you. Forget about what you think ... it is actually all about what the customers who underpin your sustainability think;

it's also about what your people who implement and execute your business model think; it's also about your supply chain's reaction; and what your external finance and risk partners think in relation to ongoing support, for example. Consider what will happen if you lose that commercial momentum.

Successful interventions will enhance your reputation. They will indicate to the world that you are in front of the game, that you are agile and that you are willing and able to optimise a dynamic business environment.

When I was dealing with post-GFC fall out, the period following government stimulus programs when the pipeline had dried up, competition had intensified, and the supply chain became even more unreliable than it already was, we were close to becoming a statistic.

We had six projects in distress – losing money and substantially delayed – and we had subcontractors queuing up to renegotiate terms. Clients were worried we would be another GFC casualty, our staff were worried about their livelihood, and we were managing cashflow daily. We posted our first ever loss. It was $5M.

Fundamental to our turnaround strategy was empowering our frontline leaders and mobilising our troops. We were at war. We co-created our intervention according to the external environment and held ourselves accountable to these measures of success weekly.

A key contributor to our success was taking our accountability to the next level through sharing our turnaround strategy with our partners. On a monthly basis we routinely site-walked and talked with our clients about our turnaround metrics and the impact on their project. And through enlivening the previously passive relationship with our bankers, we enforced their partnership and engagement in our success. Both parties were invested beyond capital.

A pessimist may cringe at the thought of revealing problems; an optimist will see their problems as the origin of their solutions. A good strategist will use all of the resources available to them, including engaging with those stakeholders that through contract or otherwise have accumulated their own significant risk and therefore have an interest.

Not only did we achieve a $7M upside through nine months, we received considerable reputation enhancement as our clients perceived our turnaround strategy to be a significant effort and outcome, so much so that not one of the six imposed penalties for delay that could have amounted to a possible additional $3M cost – a risk we wouldn't have been able to cover.

Similarly, our banker did not impose limitations on our project security facility, and following much negotiation in fact reclassified a component of our collateral to free up future cashflow. Similar negotiations saw our insurer extend our bond facility.

Ultimately the external partnerships and goodwill that we had generated enabled the business to secure 100% of our forecast revenue prior to commencement of the next financial year, 60% of which was repeat business. This had never happened before.

DEVELOPING A TACTICAL RESPONSE PLAN

We've managed businesses through economic cycles before; however, it is the frenetic pace of change and the urgency with which we must respond that makes each challenge more and more significant from both a leadership and a sustainability perspective.

Leaders and their frontline managers can be overly consumed by the business's strategy and the business plan. That's a controversial statement in many ways, the plan being one of those things you can't live without. However, this obsession and preoccupation can lead to business paralysis, particularly in the context of a crisis, when seeing, thinking, planning and acting differently is really the key to finding a way out of troubled waters.

In times of crisis, we need a pressure relief valve.

How do we navigate the implied inflexibility of an overarching strategy or a business plan? And how do we maintain discipline across our operational fundamentals while doing so?

Regrouping, reassessing and recalibrating is a bigger piece of collaborative work that should be happening in the background; call it pre-work before transitioning to a bigger picture. It is the ultimate leader's role to mobilise a key cohort and create a shorter term, interim Tactical Response Plan to maintain momentum while ducking and weaving around whatever is thrown at the business.

From a business planning perspective, set and forget is a thing of the past.

If I was to wrap up **five fundamental crisis management lessons** I have learnt and would prioritise in any Tactical Response Plan, my list would look like this. Note it is all about the solution, not the problem:

1. **People.** If your people aren't up for the crisis then replace them; don't allow them to deplete the discretionary efforts of others. While people are your ultimate enablers they can also be your immediate derailers. Unless you tell them often what is in it for them, they will go and work with someone who will.

2. **Convergence.** Concurrent strategies are designed to provide complementary business outcomes however planning to succeed in separate and mutually exclusive relationships is no different to juggling. Simplify the end game from the start.

3. **Customer-centricity.** Authentic win–win relationships with your customers need to predate any crisis because when you are 'in deep', unless they are already engaged with you and your business, it is unlikely they will partner in your mitigation strategy.

4. **Contingency.** Even if your business performance says you don't need debt, have a comfortable debt facility in place regardless, as you don't know what could come out of left field. The ability to access and the cost of such a lifeline when deep in crisis may be a bridge too far.

5. **Resilience.** Surrounding yourself with great people is a no-brainer, however it is the commitment and resilience of your people who are often up to their necks in operational carnage that will serve as your additional motivator.

Too often, businesses just hold on and wait for things to improve, or for the business activity alone to shift the line they drew in the sand last year or last month. Meanwhile, the financial fundamentals remain constantly under pressure, the continuing viability of the business becomes questionable, and its ability to step up and out of the crisis is diminishing fast.

In creating an interim **Tactical Response Plan**, consider the following:

1. **Back to basics.** Identify the core business fundamentals critical to your immediate survival.

Generally, it is *customer*, *people* and *financial* which are the top three business imperatives relevant to crisis management. That's not to say you should forget about the other planned business objectives. Rather, when in crisis and turnaround mode, these objectives are allocated a key internal stakeholder who will delegate specific actions, accountabilities and priorities.

- **Customer** is all about maintaining engagement, optimum performance delivery, and communicating your strategy around what success looks like for your customer. The key to this being a successful objective is ensuring your performance measures are never taken from your biased internal perspective – it must be an *outside-in* customer perspective.

- Similarly, **people** is about actions that promote engagement and communication, so the key internal and external stakeholders know exactly what success looks like for them and this, in turn, incentivises their own, and ultimately the business's, performance. Success originates from unrequested discretionary efforts.

- Finally, **financial** is business-specific; however, the actions that must be targeted are the cashflow metrics. Cash is real time and critical in supporting risk mitigation strategies. For example, the supplier payments that maintain productivity, the customer receipts that support operations, and the regulatory and banking covenants that underpin it all.

2. **Fixed milestones.** As these objectives dictate short-term, targeted, survival-orientated actions, compressed timeframes are critical in gaining transformation momentum.

- Prioritise objectives and actions to be resolved within, say, a revolving 10-day, 20-day and 30-day timeframe.
- Establish a succinct one-page document with clear objectives, actions, accountabilities, and measurements that progress through this 30-day cycle.
- Measure the Tactical Response Plan's performance weekly. It is pointless assessing actions not achieved that are 10 days overdue because then it is hardly tactical, and it is – more than likely – too late.

The message here is that preparedness and urgency are not only the keys to any redirection or intervention – they need to become your new business as usual.

Ultimately you need to ask yourself: how will I reliably and continuously feel or sense the business's operational pulse? What needs to happen next and by when?

3. **Reputation enhancement.** Another objective that's imperative in a short-term Tactical Response Plan is a dedicated initiative around reputation enhancement, driven by the ultimate leader(s). Why not leverage a successful transformation as a reputation builder?

KEEP CRISIS MANAGEMENT SIMPLE

Ultimately you need to ask yourself, how will I reliably and continuously feel or sense my business's operational pulse?

These suggested quick wins and critical interventions will optimise your crisis management response. The previous initiatives provide guidance so that if something comes out of left field, you will be armed with:

1. **Knowledge.** Critical numbers accurately assessed.

2. **Adaptability.** Streamlined systems and processes.

3. **Agility.** Able to respond quickly and meaningfully.

4. **Partners.** You will have depth in your finance and risk stakeholders, and access to diversity and options if you need it.

By applying these early interventions, you will have a clear strategy which has been designed from the *outside-in*, which in turn includes the following four key pillars:

1. **Meaningful objectives.** Deliver turnaround, rather than an operational 'to-do list'.

2. **Appropriate people.** Capability and business resources that will ensure actions bring outcomes – you will have the horsepower to deliver on strategy.

3. **Performance management.** A daily, weekly, monthly – or whatever is appropriate – regime of measuring outcome.

4. **Rigid timeframes.** To ensure the crisis is appropriately managed.

The message to reiterate is that preparedness and urgency are not only key to any redirection or intervention, but they need to also become your business as usual.

Maintaining an almost subconscious, up-to-date and realistic picture of your key financial metrics (the 'effect') provides you with the best opportunity for informed, urgent and accurate decision-making ahead of time (in relation to the 'causes').

Among day-to-day operational challenges escalated by technology, some of this 'common sense' gets obliterated, and relying on the capable, highly paid people that support you often won't change this!

As a leader, you will not know everything – and that's okay. However, you need to get yourself into this level of detail because you want to gain credibility by delivering predictable and reliable results. Too often, we see people 'holding on' for things to improve or shifting that line they drew in the sand last year or last month. Instead, be ready so that, as the one charged with the responsibility, you are aligned with the business in terms of being accurate, adaptable and agile. This is how you will generate deep insights into the most important stakeholders – your people and your customers – so you optimise and maximise crisis management.

YOUR MINDSHIFT:
Stay in front of the game

1. **Set up for success.**
   Corporate transformations have a tragic success rate, often being incorrectly diagnosed and producing irrelevant strategies or poorly implemented and failing to deliver the anticipated results.

2. **Create vision.**
   Successful leaders must create thinking momentum to develop compelling strategy, meaningful metrics, optimum execution and successful outcomes.

3. **Real data.**
   Do not make fundamental crisis management decisions based on forecast data – remember, you are in a crisis because you didn't see it coming.

4. **Cash is king.**
   Know exactly the regular cash-based metrics and productivity outcomes that will enable you to make immediate decisions, any day of the week.

5. **Accountability.**
   Mobilise your team and activate a Tactical Response Plan that will maintain momentum while ducking and weaving through whatever is thrown at the business.

6. **Core business.**
   Go back to basics and identify what is critical to immediate survival.

7. **Restructure.**
   Are you cost-cutting to temporarily inflate the bottom line and improve cashflow ... or are you restructuring to regenerate the business? Ultimately this is your crisis *why*.

8. **Agility.**
   A successful business is adaptable in terms of systems and processes, and agile in terms of cost structure.

9. **Synergy.**
   Identifying the value-add through integrating specific functions across different business units often provides a quick win and another level of people engagement through diversifying roles and responsibilities.

10. **Partners.**
    You need external financial partners ready to be on your side all the time. If you can't meet the external process with your internal governance, you are wasting your time.

NINE

MIND SHIFTS THAT WILL STOP THE BLEEDING

A WILLING ABILITY TO STEP OUTSIDE YOUR COMFORT ZONE

There are many approaches to strategic planning, such as the traditional situation–target–proposal approach or the more contemporary see–think–plan approach used to generate a collaborative plan structure.

Having discussed concepts in previous chapters around people being the ultimate enablers, that leadership is not simply a role at the top, and that successful strategy must enduringly move the organisational needle; in this chapter we bring all of this together and step you through a 7-Step method we call the MindShift Method.

A MindShift is a willing ability to step outside of your comfort zone. To see, think, plan and act differently.

In addition, you will need to bring three other 'tickets' to this game.

1. **ACE people.**

   At the core of this is our concept of ACE people that we discussed in chapter 4. Whether it be strategy origination, implementation or execution, without collective alignment, capability and engagement, the discretionary efforts required to co-create enduring business success will be futile.

   Collect a cohort of people comfortable with taking on numerous responsibilities and with varied skills who have a qualified view of the business's internal *and* external world, and a willingness to share.

   ACE people co-creating strategy

   Aligned   People who know what needs to be done and, equally, the impact of doing nothing.

Capable People who can deploy relevant thinking and skill to contribute to change.

Engaged People who take ownership and want to be responsible for change.

2. **Different perspectives.**

    The most valuable asset any strategy sensing initiative has is, quite simply, different perspectives.

    If there is no diversity in business or personal experiences, or approaches to problem solving and decision-making methods, a willingness to query and an ability to organise information, your output is hardly going to be game-changing is it?

    Truly successful businesses take their collaboration to the next level through a much wider lens of thought partnership, where analytical sits alongside innovative, factual alongside conceptual, creative alongside organised, and sequential alongside holistic thinking.

    You will not produce compelling outcomes without deep insights.

3. **An *outside-in* mindset.**

    The concept of *outside-in* is thought to derive from the 1970s management consulting phrase 'thinking outside the square', relating to thinking unconventionally and from a different perspective to solve a 'nine-dots' square puzzle. Today this phrase has evolved to that of *outside-in*, referring to the same push for a new perspective from outside of an organisation and specifically from a customer perspective.

    An *outside-in* perspective allows us to focus not only on internal resources and operations but also the impact these will have on a customer's view of what success looks like for them. It's essential that concerted effort is made to counteract the bias of the inside-out or inward-facing default position from which many organisations operate.

An *outside-in* view is a deliberate customer-centric mind shift. Using customer trends as a guide for product and service development is not as easy as it sounds, however. Data collection needs to go beyond the basics.

THE HOW-TO

Transformation is a process with key stages that must be carefully managed and many levers that must be pulled.

Each of the 7 steps that follow have been broken down so you can safely step outside your operational comfort zone, so you can optimise and maximise beyond conventional thinking. This is the *how-to* chapter.[1]

This is not a 'tick and flick' exercise. It is intended as a collaborative process led by an independent facilitator, devoid of 'workshop dominators' and designed to promote reflection and insight, to ultimately move the organisational needle.

The transformation phase that follows is a focused optimisation of your resources to maximise your strategic potential and enduring business success.

Steps 1 to 3 will **enable** strategic change, and steps 4 to 7 will **implement** it.

---

1   The complete MindShift Method, including all 7 steps that will enable you to see–think–plan, is available for you to download at www.briansands.com.au.

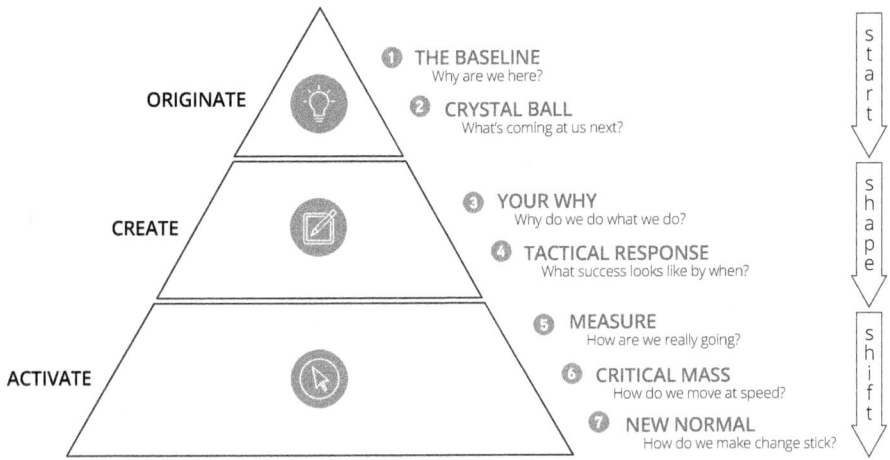

Figure 18. MindShift Thinking

Optimising and maximising through originating, creating and activating successful strategies

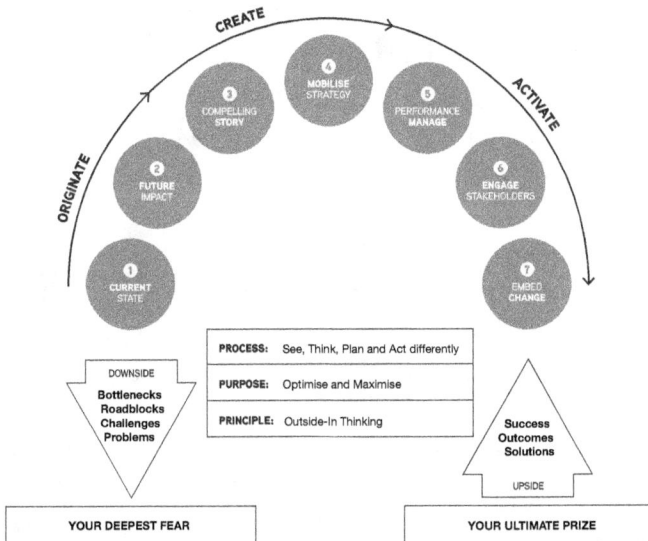

Figure 19. MindShift Doing

The 7-Step method to optimising individual thinking and transforming organisational doing

MINDSHIFT 1: THE BASELINE
Current state

Why   To set a baseline from which strategic change can occur.

What
1. Measure tangible business performance metrics now.
2. Compare the same metrics over a previous period.
3. Make comparative assessments on soft (qualitative) metrics.

How
1. Extract data from financial reports.
2. Extract data from productivity measures.
3. Consider soft metrics such as people and culture, environment and safety, corporate social impact, etc.

Output
1. Document the things the business must start, stop and keep, and:
   - do more of,
   - do less of,
   - learn, and then
   - do next.
2. Reconfirm your problem and deep fear with quantifiable data. Your starting point is now verified.

A look in the rear-view mirror, step 1 is both a qualitative (causes) and quantitative (effects) assessment drawing a line with respect to holistic performance. It is a deep dive into the causes that impact performance; that is, behaviours, systems, processes and any relevant internal resources. And to complete the impact analysis we then consider the tangible effect on business performance.

For those of you who are convinced that you already know the answer can I suggest that you immerse yourself in your cohort of ACE people and ask them what they think?

MINDSHIFT 2: CRYSTAL BALL
Future impact

Why To assess the impact of the immediate future (three years maximum) internal and external environment so as to provide a compelling response informing the strategic detail.

What 1. Consider where and to what extent your industry will shift.
2. To what extent will your offering need to adapt?
3. What will your competition look like in the future?
4. How will they be responding?

How 1. Industry data.
2. Macro-economic data.
3. Street talk.

Output Document the challenges that are outside of your control which are likely to come at you out of left field. Have your game plan in mind.

A look in the crystal ball, step 2 is a qualitative assessment of both the future internal and external environment, those factors that we can reasonably forecast as having an impact on your transformation, and what response will likely leverage this opportunity. Forewarned is forearmed.

You have performance data from step 1, you will no doubt have access to or knowledge of industry trends, and you have ACE people armed with information. Don't be too scientific nor overly prescriptive. And don't attempt to create fairy tales around what your environment will represent in three years' time. This level of strategic sensing is where we shift our thinking from short-term operational to long-term strategic. This is a critical foundation piece.

MINDSHIFT 3: YOUR WHY
Compelling story

Why   To establish your unique and compelling business proposition.

What   Articulate what success looks like.

How   Document your *why* and your *what*, through:
- Where have we come from?
- To whom do we add value?
- With what kind of services?
- What are our points of difference?
- Why do we do what we do?
- What does our success look like?

Output   1. Create your one-page *compelling story*. Include:
- your purpose
- your mission
- your values.

         2. Reconfirm your *solution* and *ultimate prize*, with forecast data.

Objectives capture the fundamental components that collectively will achieve your Purpose, described by a statement outlining a reason why. Traditional businesses will optimise *customer*, *people*, *financial*, *systems* and *product*. Progressive businesses may include *digital*, *social* and *innovation*, for example.

For example, a financial objective may be: 'We will turn around the business by restoring profitability, providing stability and a solid foundation for sustainable margin growth.' And an internal support objective may be: 'We will have a flexible organisational structure, an accurate project cost reporting system, and the right policies and procedures in place for our turnaround objectives to be enabled.'

Actions will then succinctly describe the effort – the what and the how – required to achieve the objective. Often there will be numerous actions deployed in order to achieve the one objective.

Accountability is ownership, the who. All the strategic creating initiatives will mean nothing if you are unable to execute upon each action with relevant capabilities.

Measure is the quantity, the specific and comparable business performance metric, that relates to a specific action.

Timeframe is the realistic period within which a specific action can be achieved.

* * *

In preceding chapters we discussed a number of concepts and, assuming that your values are watertight, there are three concepts that – if kept top of mind through this step 3 planning process – will enable you to optimise and maximise change:

1. Being able to distinguish your *why* from your *what*.

2. Co-creating with aligned, capable and engaged (ACE) people.

3. Understanding the reasons strategies can fail.

This fundamental step is where you really need to go into top gear to co-create creative, holistic and non-linear strategic thinking. If you can shift your mindset away from operational planning, you will have more chance of creating a unique value proposition.

We know intuitively that the motive behind an action is the most important part of any story. When it comes to your business, knowing your *why* will help you stay committed to your change objective and generate buy-in from others.

Using the detail you have extracted as a group from the preceding two steps, reflect and reassess these metrics for deep insights that will underpin – or indeed enhance – your purpose and your compelling story from your customers' perspective.

Consider these 20 questions as thought provokers; there are an almost infinite number of considerations that can and will inform your point of difference. And just a reminder: you are attempting to distinguish your *why*, not your *what*, nor your *how*.

1.   Why are we doing this?

2.   Why are we in business?

3.   Why do we exist?

4.   Why are we who we are today?

5.   What are we great at?

6.   Why are we good at what we do?

7.   What are we poor at?

8.   What do customers say about us?

9.   Why do we offer this product?

10. What do we offer next?

11. Do we give back?

12. What is our social impact?

13. Are our values real?

14. What is our environmental impact?

15. What is compelling to others?

16. What is compelling to us?

17. What are our best behaviours?

18. Do our values relate to our impacts?

19. What are our worst behaviours?

20. Do we do what we say?

The output from this step informs the operational response in the following steps that will move the needle. There is a reason that there is 'a bit' to this step.

MINDSHIFT 4: TACTICAL RESPONSE
Mobilise strategy

Why   1. To create an operational response that defines the resources required to enable and ensure strategic change.
         2. To put a plan around business sustainability.

What   Create the strategy – a specific plan of action, the framework and metrics that define transformation.

How   Document your how:
- a finite number of relevant objectives
- no more than three actions for each objective
- a quantifiable measure of success for each action.

Output   Create a strategy document, your operational response.

This is the momentum builder, the mechanics behind your compelling reason for being in business. Importantly, this is not only a 'clear lens' on your internal operations, it is a 'clean slate' into the external relationships and resources that through partnership will enable you to enduringly move the organisational needle.

Assuming you have all of the internal resources and external relationships you require to optimise strategic change is delusional. You have committed to a process of improvement. Everything should be up for grabs. Perhaps not all resources will require fundamental change, however the opportunity you have embraced of seeing, thinking, planning and acting differently will at least tweak at the edges, if not originate new ways of doing.

MINDSHIFT 5: MEASURE
Performance manage

Why   To regularly measure performance so as to ensure achievement, and so as to remain agile and adaptable to the dynamic environment.

What   1. Ensure business performance improvement is achieved.
2. Prioritise actions and activities.
3. Align internal capability to operational tasks.
4. Seek out external resources that will add value.
5. Identify capability and resource gaps.

How   1. Data collection.
2. Personal interaction.
3. Accountability for each activity.
4. A quantifiable measure of success for each.
5. A timeframe within which to deliver each.

Output The outputs of steps 3 and 4 have captured the metrics and set expectations around timeframes; the output of step 5 will be your business-unique method such as a live dashboard that will manage achieving those metrics.

A regular forum of reporting outcomes, sharing experiences, celebrating successes, learning from mistakes, reassessing priorities and deploying additional support – for example – will be a 'best for business' process that you will co-create internally. Consider as a step 5 action designing a different method of collaboration that utilises technology for data collection and sharing, and a more engaging collaboration that will leverage shared experiences. Mind-numbing reviews of previous reports and copious note taking and recording minutes are hardly innovative.

Agility and adaptability will be key to maintaining discretionary effort and change momentum. Be prepared to make tough decisions. Be prepared to make capability changes. Be aware of the consequences of holding on, but also be aware of the impact of looking for the silver bullet when things don't seem to be going your way. In either case, change fatigue is the strategy killer.

Conversely, giving importance to and celebrating achievement will be the fuel for ongoing discretionary effort despite the dynamics of the changing environment you are creating.

MINDSHIFT 6: CRITICAL MASS
Engage stakeholders

Why   To tell 'everyone' why we are doing what we are doing so that they know how strategic change will add value to them, and in turn, so that they will return discretionary effort to our cause.

What
1. Define internal and external stakeholders.
2. Articulate what's in it for them – individually and collectively.
3. Allocate accountability to managing stakeholder groups.

How
1. Communication.
2. Performance – action not words.
3. Tangible value adding.

Output
1. Design your Social Network Analysis to outline the key touchpoints within both your internal and external stakeholder environment.
2. Communicate the value you will add to whom, where and by when. And communicate it again when you have delivered it.
3. Create subtle collaboration strategies, partnerships that through the normal course will add momentum to:
   - change initiatives
   - performance improvement
   - credibility.

MINDSHIFT 7: NEW NORMAL
Embed change

Why   To ensure that stakeholders are engaged in the holistic change process so that discretionary efforts continue to deliver enduring upside.

What
1. People are willing and able.
2. Business is agile and adaptable.
3. A repeatable new way of doing.

How
1. Analysing the how with data – what is working, what is not.
2. Rewarding compliance and achievement.
3. Creating a culture of success by improvement.

Output
1. Document the changes that you need to step through, defined by the 'shift' your strategy has impacted on the previous organisational structure.
2. Where was the pain? And where is the gain?

While this entire **MindShift** method could be described as an incremental change management process, this final step 7 is the mechanism for maintaining the new and improved business environment. This is how you ensure exponential.

Be aware, however, of the concept of *change failure*, brought about by:

- allowing too much complexity

- failing to build a coalition

- not having a clear picture of what success looks like

- poor communication

- allowing roadblocks to accumulate

- not planning for quick wins

- declaring victory too soon

- failing to anchor changes at the top.

WHAT SUCCESS LOOKS LIKE

A successful transformation will enhance the capability of leaders and the culture of business leadership across the board, and in doing so it will create momentum for an authentic group of followers. This is where you will quantify the success of your transformation process. Collecting the right information and data is critical in terms of managing change and measuring the success of it.

Ask yourself these 10 questions and answer with the real data you now have. To be enduringly successful, you need to have achieved all 10.

1. **Resolution.** Have we transformed our *problem* into our *solution*? Do we have a sustainable business model?

2. **Performance.** Is there distinctive business performance upside? Have we moved the needle?

3. **Compelling.** From an *outside-in* perspective, do we have a compelling proposition? Why do we do what we do?

4. **Alignment.** Do our values align with our purpose?

5. **Sustainable.** Have we created a niche and/or created new opportunity?

6. **Opportunity.** Can we quantify what success looks like by when and for how long? At what point will the next business horizon(s) likely materialise?

7. **Capability.** Do we have more ACE people now than when we started this process?

8. **Innovation.** Do we have both people capability and business capacity to innovate? Are we constantly on the lookout?

9. **Leverage.** Are external stakeholders on board, and are they invested? Are we optimising and maximising them?

10. **Data driven.** Are we extending our thinking and doing through collecting, analysing and leveraging deep data?

CONCLUSION
GETTING THROUGH TO
THE OTHER SIDE

You have read throughout that we had some very tough times during the Global Financial Crisis. It was frightening. We must remember that the world was falling apart, banks were filing for bankruptcy.

Despite the high-value learning that has enabled me to do what I do today, the precarious financial position that was imposed on us back then could have been catastrophic. It's not simply about a business being unsuccessful, losing money and closing the doors. It is a much deeper consideration around 'survival anxiety' brought about by providing and then protecting a massive net-work of personal livelihoods, both directly and indirectly.

As a company director I took very seriously obligations to prevent insolvent trading, and did have discussions around whether we would have to close the doors. We needed to have those discus-sions. It was our burning platform.

In fear of self-promotion however, I didn't think we *wouldn't* survive, it was more a matter of how much it was going to hurt and what it was going to look like on the other side.

The whole premise around *Stop The Bleeding* is a phrase that came to mind back then, one I verbalised regularly as I watched

$5M leave the business over the initial two-month period. Fortunately, I also watched one million dollars come back into the business in seven of the nine months that followed.

During this period, we backed ourselves into succeeding, and before we had achieved it, we had established a business development strategy on the basis of impending turnaround success. The lever I had always relied upon was reputation. I made sure that in spite of my survival anxiety, each client knew without question that we had a turnaround strategy and a sustainable end game. I exposed myself and the business to external measurement against these project specific strategies, every month.

This reputational success led to us securing 100% of the future year's budgeted revenue before the end of the following Q1. Coming off a turnaround year, this next one was about transformation – doing more with less essentially, a lean overhead structure supported by a more relevant project governance. Margins were under pressure through a deep red ocean of competition, however we had risk management well and truly covered.

I was exhausted by this time. The relentless business survival game face was taking its toll on both my enthusiasm for work and my happiness contribution at home. I decided that it was time to go, so I sat down with my two business partners and agreed an exit later that year that included shaping a business they wanted to carry forward. That final year then became the consolidation year, when we remodelled a business of reduced scale so as to mitigate the lumpiness and uncertainty of a highly competitive and crowded market.

When I departed on 30 June 2013 we had secured the budgeted revenue for the next year. The business was well and truly set up for success once again.

Ironically, after a short time 'out' in contract roles with Broad Constructions and Leighton Contractors, I decided I wanted to get back into the cut and thrust of business problem solving. That was my *next*. And it is still my *now*, and probably will be for some time.

BEING ALERT TO CRISIS

Global political tensions have been escalating for years, particularly among the so-called superpowers. Digital disruption, and the pace of change, will never be this slow again. Inside this global pressure cooker, the world has been 'holding on' economically for some time and, as I write this, the COVID-19 pandemic has tipped us over the edge.

There has been a wariness in financial markets since the GFC. Business leaders have been forecasting market contraction for some time. Many economists are claiming recession is here and others are saying it is close. There is no doubt it's headed our way and the impact will be extensive, delivering considerable collateral damage.

Domestically, governments are deploying financial stimulus as quickly as humanly possible, however that may not necessarily be your silver bullet. For the most part these packages provide cost relief via credit extensions and deferment of financial liabilities. They say it's about hibernation. But be aware, if you hibernate you will be a long way behind those that innovate during such times, as it's highly likely that hibernation – if you choose that path – could be a two-year slumber.

Whether you are faced with immediate crisis management or you see one coming, the effectiveness of your response starts with your headspace. Often, we need to force a mind shift rather than experience an event in order to start seeing, thinking, planning and acting differently – to make that quantum leap away from 'holding on'.

When faced with a crisis, your turnaround strategy needs to be specific, high impact and without delay. You need to be on your game, with your best internal team and external advisors. However, before you come out all guns blazing and exposing yourself to further risk, consider these **five fundamental crisis-ready self-reflections** that will prepare you for crisis leadership:

1. Why am I doing this? Is my compelling reason for being in business a proposition that delivers meaning and purpose to me?

2. Where is my headspace at? If it is a one-dimensional fight-to-the-death 'mentality' then I am on a hiding to nothing, so what is my end game?

3. What is my pressure relief valve? What am I doing each and every day to reset my physical and mental self? What is my daily ritual of mental clarity? How do I *cool the jets*?

4. To avoid the same old people doing the same old thing and 'holding on' for a better outcome, how do I ensure I have *can*, *know* and *want* people in the trenches alongside me?

5. Do I have an independent external advisor I can rely on who can co-create crisis management, and who is prepared to get *down and dirty* with me and open doors that I cannot get near?

This is the psychological foundation that will enable you to stop the bleeding. Without it you may succeed in stemming the flow, however the bleeding never stops.

A NEW PERSPECTIVE

There is immense value in seeking, receiving and coordinating different perspectives. It is fundamental to authentically seeing, thinking, planning and acting differently. It is the foundation for the transition from a fixed mindset to a growth mindset, and the quantum leap to a shared mindset.

Perspective is the way we see the world. It comes from our individual point of view, influenced by our experiences, our personal values, our current state of mind, and the assumptions or preconceptions we bring into a situation, among a whole lot of other things.

Perspective-taking is *reactive*; it is putting yourself in someone else's shoes, it is about being able to understand a concept from an alternative point of view, enabling us to explore a previous situation, better appreciate feelings, convey empathy or inform decision-making.

Perspective-seeking is *proactive*; it is about being curious through asking for a point of view so you can better understand a specific situation. It's about asking for an opinion to potentially unlock your perspective, however the trap is seeking advice from people who have the same point of view as you in order to validate your decision-making. Authentically it is about removing a blind spot or filling a knowledge void.

Perspective coordination is the co-creation that we often refer to, the ability to collate observations and create a much bigger and richer picture.

What did you learn that was important to others yet not considered by you? What did you learn about others? What do you now understand about the situation and how has your perspective changed? What do you see differently? Do you need more information before you make a decision? Will your decision be different than originally intended? Can you quantify a collective upside from a coordinated perspective? How will your decision impact others? How do you now need to communicate differently?

We often exist inside an organisational pressure cooker. An environment where perhaps the pace of change is our excuse for not taking the time to step back and take a different perspective. When competing in this fast lane, people often confuse perspective with reality, and struggle to truly understand the point of view of others.

A perspective is not right or wrong, however our perspectives shape how we act or react in any given situation.

I don't believe that my perception is my reality. I do believe however that the more perspectives I get, the closer to reality I may get.

www.ingramcontent.com/pod-product-compliance
Lightning Source LLC
Chambersburg PA
CBHW061020220326
41597CB00016BB/1716